THE COMPLETE POEMS OF
RICHARD ALDINGTON

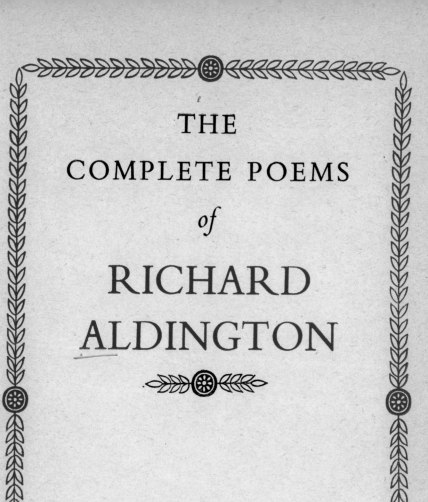

THE
COMPLETE POEMS
of
RICHARD
ALDINGTON

ALLAN WINGATE
LONDON

First published mcmxlviii
by Allan Wingate (Publishers) Limited
64 Great Cumberland Place London W1

Set in Monotype Bembo type
and printed in Great Britain by
Tonbridge Printers Ltd
Tonbridge

CONTENTS

8

BIBLIOGRAPHICAL NOTE

SOME of these poems first appeared in the Imagist Anthologies, 1914, 1915, 1916, 1917. The first of these was published by A. & C. Boni, New York, and the Poetry Bookshop, London. The others were published by Houghton Mifflin, Boston, and Constable & Co, London.

Images (1910–1915): London, the Poetry Bookshop, 1915

Images, Old and New: Boston, Four Seas Co, 1916

Images (second, enlarged edition): London, the Egoist Press, 1919 (re-issued by Allen and Unwin)

Images of War (Limited edition, with decorations by Paul Nash): London, Beaumont Press, 1919

Images of War (new, enlarged edition): London, Allen and Unwin, 1919

Images of Desire: London, Elkin Mathews, 1919 (re-issued by Allen and Unwin)

War and Love (contains most of the poems published in England in 'Images of War' and 'Images of Desire'): Boston, Four Seas Co, 1919

Exile and Other Poems: London, Allen and Unwin, 1923

Exile and Other Poems: New York, Dial Press, 1923

A Fool i' the Forest: London, Allen and Unwin, 1925

A Fool i' the Forest: New York, Dial Press, 1925

A Dream in the Luxembourg: Chatto and Windus, 1930

Love and the Luxembourg: Limited Edition, Covici, Friede, Inc., 1930

The Eaten Heart and Other Poems: Chatto and Windus, 1933

The Eaten Heart and Other Poems: Doubleday Doran, 1933

Life Quest: Chatto and Windus, 1935

Life Quest: Doubleday Doran, 1935

The Crystal World: Heinemann, 1937

The Crystal World: Doubleday Doran, 1937

Reprints, special editions and collected editions are not included in this list.

ACKNOWLEDGEMENTS

THE author wishes to thank Sir Stanley Unwin and Messrs Allen & Unwin for permission to include in this complete edition the poems published by them under the titles of *Images, Images of War, Images of Desire, Exile* and *A Fool i' the Forest*; Mr A. S. Frere, C.B.E., and Messrs Heinemann for *A Dream in the Luxembourg, The Eaten Heart, Life Quest,* and *The Crystal World*. Acknowledgements are also due to 'Queen's Quarterly' for *A Grave*; 'Poetry Magazine' for *Dilemma*; 'Yale Review' for *Life Goes On*; the 'Saturday Review of Literature' for *January Aconites*; the 'Forum' for *A Place of Young Pines* and *To One Dead*; the 'North American Review' for *Morning in the South*.

INTRODUCTION

MORE than thirty-five years have passed since the first three poems in this book were published in Chicago by Miss Harriet Monroe in her magazine *Poetry*. If anyone is curious to know why the poems of a nineteen-year-old English boy first appeared in Chicago, I can speedily enlighten him. In 1912 no English periodical would publish such writing, and I happened to know Mr Ezra Pound, who was busy inspiring Miss Monroe and founding one of his biannual poetical 'movements'. The numbers of *Poetry* afforded the columnists of those days a deal of mirth of a good-natured kind, and intentionally or unintentionally they informed the outer world of the existence of what was then called 'the new poetry'. I was annoyed with those columnists at the time, but I see now that they were useful allies.

The beginning of the 'new poetry' or of 'modernist poetry' or whatever you choose to call it is generally placed in that year, 1912. Let me say at once and firmly that I claim no share whatever in the so-called 'revolution of 1912'. It was a mere accident that what I was writing then chanced to meet with the approval of the verse revolutionaries, just as the publication of the poems in America was an accident. I am not ambitious to be known as the introducer or part introducer of some novelty in writing. There are two sorts of originality, the conscious and the unconscious. The former consists in doing for the first time something nobody else has thought of, which anybody can imitate. The latter consists in doing something which nobody else can do, and that is inimitable.

Commentators on verse are usually more interested in discussing what they call 'tendencies' and elaborating their own theories than in studying the work of the individual poet. Moreover, anthologists have the very bad habit of choosing from former anthologies (there are exceptions) instead of making their own choice. For this and for other reasons, my poems have been known (in so far as they have been known at all) almost entirely by a few stock poems selected from what I wrote before I was twenty-one. This is rather depressing, and I hope that the publication of this volume will induce a few readers to explore a little further.

Willy-nilly I have been associated with the 'revolt of 1912', and I think it appropriate to say a few words to dissociate myself from attitudes towards poetry which are not mine. I have already implied that I do not believe in willed or self-conscious 'originality'. I do not believe either that poetry is a matter of technique. Naturally I know that technique is important, but I do not believe that Milton wrote *Paradise Lost* solely or chiefly to produce and perfect a certain type of blank verse. The triumph of technical skill is that it should be un-obtrusive—which does not mean that I defend sloppy, careless, or ignorant writing. But there is a cant about 'style' and 'tech-nique' I find offensive.

Again, there is the intellectualist cant, or what might be called the 'highbrow' fallacy in poetry. 'Highbrow' is a danger-ous word to use, and I must try to make my position quite clear. In a mere altercation between lowbrows and highbrows I should have to take my stand with the highbrows, since my whole experience of life tells me that some men and women are much more highly gifted than the majority—in other words, an élite does exist. I have no sympathy with those who throw the word 'highbrow' at anybody who happens to be a little more educated than they are. On the other hand, the word 'highbrow' so exactly hits off the pretentiousness of a certain type of intellectual that it oughtn't to be lost. I suggest that there are three main traits by which the highbrow may be recognised. First, he is one who through some defect of the soul values the letter of knowledge more than its spirit. Second, he is terribly over-anxious to be sure that he is 'admiring the right thing', and by the 'right thing' he really means whatever is approved by the little group to which he happens to belong. Third, he is one who falsely thinks himself superior to other men and women merely on the grounds stated above; the intellectual snob.

Much of the intellectualist poetry of our time comes from persons of this type. Obviously, poetry has intellectual elements, but it is not solely intellectual. Men and women are not distinguished from one another only by quality of mind, but also by the quality of their feelings and the quality of their senses. And all these qualities must be present in poetry, though I don't for a moment believe there is any fixed or ideal ratio. Many Japanese poems are almost unalloyed sense impressions; the Portuguese *Cantigas d'Amigo* are very nearly unalloyed feeling; and the poem of Lucretius is a very intellectual performance. In Shakespeare, mind, senses, and feeling are all represented with uncommon intensity in varying proportions. If there is an art of pure intellect, absolutely divorced from the feelings and senses, it is not poetry, but mathematics.

Again, the sensual and emotional qualities distinguish poetry from philosophy, for though philosophy undoubtedly takes account of both, it is not concerned directly with the life of the senses and the feelings, but with abstractions derived from them. Thus poetry can never be wholly philosophical, though there may be, perhaps must be, some philosophy in it. I believe that Mr A. E. Housman was expressing a valuable truth when in his famous lecture he laid stress on the physical basis of poetry and on its spontaneity.

This brings up the interesting questions: How do people write poetry? Where does it 'come from'? Is there such a thing as 'inspiration'? I confess I am quite unable to answer these questions. But, speaking from my own experience, I find it to a great extent similar to Mr Housman's, in the sense that poetry (by which I mean what I have sometimes dared to hope might be poetry) was not the result of self-conscious effort, but seemed to occur quite spontaneously and mysteriously. There is a sensation that somebody else's voice has spoken. That is the moment of poetic ecstasy, which almost invariably occurs in a mood of what Wordsworth called 'wise passivity'—all the rest is hard work.

This brings me to two other elements of poetry about which I feel great diffidence in speaking—I mean reverence and the sense of mystery. By 'reverence' I understand no false or affected humility, but an intimate and spontaneous conviction that what is not me, what is outside me, is far greater and more interesting than I am, although the only account I can give of it is how it appears to me and through me. By the sense of mystery I understand the experience of certain places and times when one's whole nature seems to be in touch with a presence, a *genius loci*, a potency. I won't go into the psychology of this or even attempt to argue that it may not be a self-induced delusion. I shall only say that the experience seems to have occurred to many other people in many ages, and add that when I use the word 'god' or 'gods' or the name of some Hellenic deity, I am not indulging in a mythological flourish but refer to the actual experience of some 'potency'. I have tried to describe some of these experiences in my novel, *All Men Are Enemies*.

One more point. Though I believe that a poet should make use of any knowledge he may have, all parade of erudition is abhorrent to me. There are only one or two translations in this volume. My translations of foreign poets are collected in two books (in England) called *Medallions* and *Fifty Romance Poems*. There is one passage of 'A Fool i' th' Forest', written in French because it happened to come that way, but otherwise there are only a few words of foreign languages. As early as 1912 I used the device of the unacknowledged quotation with an ironical twist, but the reader will not find many instances. The most frequent are in 'A Fool i' th' Forest' and range from Sappho to Renan. In 'A Dream in the Luxembourg' it only occurs once. Otherwise everything in this book is my own, and at

16

any rate not consciously derived or paraphrased from other writers.

But come, this is dry work (as Mr Smangle observed on another occasion), let us rinse our mouths with a drop of sherry. I hope what I have written above does not sound pretentious—it is meant humbly enough. Everyone writing about poetry in the abstract tends to be a little solemn and pompous. And (it seems often to be forgotten) a poet is one who produces poems, not one who holds sound or original views about how poetry ought to be written. At all events, what I have written here is intended only to indicate the sort of ideal at which I aimed in attempting this most difficult and rare art. In no sense does this introduction claim that I have ever reached that ideal or anything near it. Make no mistake about that. I make no claim for the following pages except that I have done my best and have tried not to be false to my ideals. I can only submit them to the public judgment without defiance and without apology, in the belief that in the main that judgment is a just one.

RICHARD ALDINGTON

IMAGES

CHORICOS

THE ancient songs
Pass deathward mournfully.

Cold lips that sing no more, and withered wreaths,
Regretful eyes, and drooping breasts and wings—
Symbols of ancient songs,
Mournfully passing
Down to the great white surges,
Watched of none
Save the frail sea-birds
And the lithe pale girls,
Daughters of Oceanus.

And the songs pass from the green land
Which lies upon the waves as a leaf
On the flowers of hyacinths.
And they pass from the waters,
The manifold winds and the dim moon,
And they come
Silently winging through soft Cimmerian dusk,
To the quiet level lands
That she keeps for us all,
That she wrought for us all for sleep
In the silver days of the earth's dawning—
Proserpina, daughter of Zeus.

And we turn from the Cyprian's breasts,
And we turn from thee,
Phoebus Apollo,
And we turn from the music of old,
And the hills that we loved and the meads,
And we turn from the fiery day,
And the lips that were over-sweet;
For silently

Brushing the fields with red-shod feet,
With purple robe
Searing the grass as with a sudden flame,
Death,
Thou hast come upon us.
And of all the ancient songs
Passing to the swallow-blue halls
By the dark streams of Persephone,
This only remains—
That in the end we turn to thee,
Death,
We turn to thee, singing
One last song.

O death,
Thou art an healing wind
That blowest over white flowers
A-tremble with dew;
Thou art a wind flowing
Over far leagues of lonely sea;
Thou art the dusk and the fragrance;
Thou art the lips of love mournfully smiling;
Thou art the sad peace of one
Satiate with old desires;
Thou art the silence of beauty,
And we look no more for the morning,
We yearn no more for the sun
Since with thy white hands,
Death,
Thou crownest us with the pallid chaplets,
The slim colourless poppies
Which in thy garden alone
Softly thou gatherest.

And silently;
And with slow feet approaching—

And with bowed head and unlit eyes,
We kneel before thee;
And thou, leaning towards us,
Caressingly layest upon us
Flowers from thy thin cold hands,
And, smiling as a chaste woman
Knowing love in her heart,
Thou seelest our eyes
And the illimitable quietude
Comes gently upon us.

TO A GREEK MARBLE

POTNIA, Potnia,
White grave goddess,
Pity my sadness,
O silence of Paros.

I am not of these about thy feet,
These garments and decorum;
I am thy brother,
Thy lover of aforetime crying to thee,
And thou hearest me not.

I have whispered thee in thy solitudes
Of our loves in Phrygia,
The far ecstasy of burning noons
When the fragile pipes
Ceased in the cypress shade,
And the brown fingers of the shepherd
Moved over slim shoulders;
And only the cicada sang.

I have told thee of the hills
And the lisp of reeds
And the sun upon thy breasts.
And thou hearest me not,
Potnia, Potnia,
Thou hearest me not.

ARGYRIA

O YOU,
O you most fair,
Swayer of reeds, whisperer
Among the flowering rushes,
You have hidden away your hands
Beneath the poplar leaves;
You have given them to the white waters.

Swallow-fleet,
Sea-child cold from waves;
Slight reed that sang so blithely in the wind;
White cloud the white sun kissed into the air;
Pan mourns for you.

White limbs, white song,
Pan mourns for you.

AT MITYLENĒ

O Artemis,
Will you not leave the dark fastness
And set your steel-white foot upon the foam,
And come across the rustling sand
Setting it adrift with the wind of your raiment.

For these women have laid out a purple cloth,
And they have builded you an altar
Of white shells for the honey.
They have taken the sea grass for garlands
And cleansed their lips with the sea.

O Artemis,
Girdle the gold about you,
Set the silver upon your hair
And remember us—
We, who have grown weary even of music,
We, who would scream behind the wild dogs of
    Scythia.

STELE

Pan, O Pan,
The oread weeps in the stony olive-garden
On the hillside.

There bloom the fragile
Blue-purple wind-flowers,
There the wild fragrant narcissus
Bends by the grey stones.

But Pan, O Pan,
The oread weeps in the stony olive-garden;
She heeds not the moss-coloured lizards
And crocus-yellow butterflies.

For her reed-pipe
That was the crying of the wind,
Her pipe that was the singing
Wind of the mountain,
Her pipe is broken.

Pan, O Pan,
As you rush from the peaks
With the wood-girls and flower-girls
And the shouting fauns,
Unawares you have broken her little reed
With your stamping hoofs.

And she weeps in the olive-garden.

LESBIA

Grow weary if you will, let me be sad.
Use no more speech now;
Let the silence spread gold hair above us,
Fold on delicate fold.
Use no more speech;
You had the ivory of my life to carve. . . .

And Picus of Mirandola is dead;
And all the gods they dreamed and fabled of,
Hermes and Thoth and Christ are rotten now,
Rotten and dank. . . .
And through it all I see your pale Greek face;
Tenderness
Makes me as eager as a little child to love you,
You morsel left half-cold on Cæsar's plate.

LEMURES

In Nineveh,
And beyond Nineveh
In the dusk
They were afraid.

In Thebes of Egypt
In the dusk
They chanted of them to the dead.

In my Lesbos and Achaia
Where the Gods dwelt
We knew them.

Now men say 'They are not';
But in the dusk
Ere the white sun comes—
A gay child that bears a white candle—
I am afraid of their rustling,
Of their terrible silence,
The menace of their secrecy.

HERMES, LEADER OF THE DEAD

WE who loved thy lyre,
Yet knew the end of all songs
A lamentation and a mourning;
We, who loved Eos—
That maiden whiter than Narcissus—
And loved the midday heat, the sea-winds
Rustling across the vineyards;
Now in the twilight
Hold forth trembling hands
To thee, Hermes,
Leader of the Dead.

Bear us upon thy wingèd flight
Down the dark blue ways unto Orcus;
Make us stabile
With thy imperishable hands,
For our feet stumble, and age
Loosens our knees;
Our wearied eyes
Yearn for the heavy bowed gold blossoms
Beneath the very grey sky
Of Persephone.

THE RIVER

1

I HAVE drifted along the river
Until I moored my boat
By these crossed trunks.
Here the mist moves
Over fragile leaves and rushes,
Colourless waters and brown fading hills.

You have come from beneath the trees
And move within the mist,
A floating leaf.

2

O blue flower of the evening,
You have touched my face
With your leaves of silver.

Love me, for I must depart.

EPIGRAMS

NEW LOVE

She has new leaves
After her dead flowers,
Like the little almond tree
Which the frost hurt.

OCTOBER

The beech-trees are silver
For lack of the tree's blood;
At your kiss my lips
Became like the silver beech-leaves.

A GIRL

You were that clear Sicilian fluting
That pains our thought even now.

You were the notes
Of cold fantastic grief
Some few found beautiful.

BEAUTY,
THOU HAST HURT ME OVERMUCH

THE light is a wound to me.
The soft notes
Feed upon the wound.

Where wert thou born
O thou woe
That consumest my life?
Whither comest thou?

Toothed wind of the seas,
No man knows thy beginning.
As a bird with strong claws
Thou woundest me,
O beautiful sorrow.

IN THE OLD GARDEN

I HAVE sat here happy in the garden,
Watching the still pool and the reeds
And the dark clouds
Which the wind of the upper air
Tore like the green leafy boughs
Of the divers-hued trees of late summer;
But though I greatly delight
In these and the water-lilies,
That which sets me nighest to weeping
Is the rose and white colour of the smooth
    flagstones,
And the pale yellow grasses
Among them.

JUNE RAIN

HOT, a griffin's mouth of flame,
The sun rasped with his golden tongue
The city streets, till men and walls shrivelled;
The dusty air stagnated.

At the third noon a wind rippled,
A wide sea silently breaking;
A thin veil of rain-drops
Hid the sun and the hard blue.

A grey garment of rain,
Cold as hoar frost in April
Enwrapped us.

O DAUGHTER of Isis,
Thou standest beside the wet highway
Of this decayed Rome,
A manifest harlot.
Straight and slim art thou
As a marble phallus;
Thy face is the face of Isis
—Carven
As she is carven in basalt.
And my heart stops with awe
At the presence of gods,
For there beside thee on the stall of images
Is the head of Osiris
Thy lord.

AMALFI

WE will come down to you,
O very deep sea,
And drift upon your pale green waves
Like scattered petals.

We will come down to you from the hills,
From the scented lemon-groves,
From the hot sun.
We will come down,
O Thalassa,
And drift upon
Your pale green waves
Like petals.

BROMIOS

THE withered bonds are broken.
The waxed reeds and the double pipe
Clamour about me;
The hot wind swirls
Through the red pine trunks.

Io! The fauns and the satyrs.
The touch of their shagged curled fur
And blunt horns.
They have wine in heavy craters
Painted black and red;
Wine to splash on her white body.

Io!
She shrinks from the cold shower—
Afraid, afraid!
Let the Maenads break through the myrtles
And the boughs of the rhododaphnai.
Let them tear the quick deer's flesh.
Ah, the cruel exquisite fingers.

Io!
I have brought you the brown clusters,
The ivy-boughs and pine-cones.
Your breasts are cold sea-ripples,
But they smell of the warm grasses.
Throw wide the chiton and the peplum,
Maidens of the dew,
Beautiful are your bodies, O Maenads,
Beautiful the sudden folds,

The vanishing curves of the white linen
About you.

Io!
Hear the rich laughter of the forest,
The cymbals,
The trampling of the panisks and the centaurs.

IMAGES

1

LIKE a gondola of green scented fruits
Drifting along the dark canals of Venice,
You, O exquisite one,
Have entered into my desolate city.

2

The blue smoke leaps
Like swirling clouds of birds vanishing,
So my love leaps towards you,
Vanishes and is renewed.

3

A rose-yellow moon in a pale sky
When the sunset is faint vermilion
In the mist among the tree-boughs
Art thou to me, my beloved.

4

A young beech-tree on the edge of the forest
Stands still in the evening,
Yet shudders through all its leaves in the light air
And seems to fear the stars—
So are you still and so tremble.

5

The red deer are high on the mountain,
They are beyond the last pine-trees,
And my desires have run with them.

6

The flower which the wind has shaken
Is soon filled again with rain:
So does my heart fill slowly with tears
Until you return.

THE FAUN
SEES SNOW FOR THE FIRST TIME

Zeus,
Brazen-thunder-hurler,
Cloud-whirler, son-of-Kronos,
Send vengeance on these Oreads
Who strew
White frozen flecks of mist and cloud
Over the brown trees and the tufted grass
Of the meadows, where the stream
Runs black through shining banks
Of bluish white.

Zeus,
Are the halls of heaven broken up
That you flake down upon me
Feather-strips of marble?

Dis and Styx!
When I stamp my hoof
The frozen-cloud-specks jam into the cleft
So that I reel upon two slippery points. . . .

Fool, to stand here cursing
When I might be running!

REFLECTIONS

1

Steal out with me
Over the moss and the daffodils.
Come to the temple,
Hung with sprays from untrimmed hedges.

I bring you a token
From the golden-haired revellers,
From the mad procession.

Come,
Flute girls shall pipe to us—
Their beautiful fingers!—
They are yellow-throated birds,
They send perfumes from dawn-scented
    garments,
Bending above us.

Come,
Bind your hair with white poplar,
Let your lips be sweet
Wild roses of Pæstum.

2

Ghost moths hover over asphodel;
Shades, once Lais' peers
Drift past us;
The mist is grey.

Far over us
The white wave-crests flash in the sun;
The sea-girls lie upon hot weedy rocks.

Now the Maid returns to us
With fragrance of the world
And of the hours of gods.

On earth
Apple-trees, weighted with red fruit,
Streams, passing through the corn-lands,
Hear laughter.

3
We pluck the asphodel,
Yet we weave no crowns
For we have no vines;
No one speaks here;
No one kisses.

SUMMER

A BUTTERFLY,
Black and scarlet,
Spotted with white,
Fans its wings
Over a privet flower.

A thousand crimson foxgloves,
Tall bloody pikes,
Stand motionless in the gravel quarry;
The wind runs over them.

A rose film over a pale sky
Fantastically cut by dark chimneys;
Candles winking in the windows
Across an old city garden.

SCENTS

WHITE JONQUILS

OLD cloisters where a hollow fountain drips
And the brown church walls
Are soft with summer sun.

And the moist garden mould in March
After the wind.

YELLOW JONQUILS

The moon
Low down the hills Sorrento sees about her—
The orange orchards sweet in May.
Again the soft wet earth
In English gardens
When the rain and wind have passed.

THE POPLAR

WHY do you always stand there shivering
Between the white stream and the road?

The people pass through the dust
On bicycles, in carts, in motor cars;
The waggoners go by at dawn;
The lovers walk on the grass path at night.
Stir from your roots, walk, poplar!
You are more beautiful than they are.

I know that the white wind loves you,
Is always kissing you, and turning up
The white lining of your green petticoat.
The sky darts through you like blue rain,
And the grey rain drips on your flanks
And loves you.
And I have seen the moon
Slip his silver penny into your pocket
As you straightened your hair;
And the white mist curling and hesitating
Like a bashful lover about your knees.

I know you, poplar;
I have watched you since I was ten.
But if you had a little real love,
A little strength,
You would leave your nonchalant idle lovers
And go walking down the white road
Behind the waggoners.

There are beautiful beeches down beyond the hill.
Will you always stand there shivering?

SHE is all so slight
And tender and white
  As a May morning.
She walks without hood
At even. It is good
  To hear her sing.

It is God's will
That I shall love her still
  As he loves Mary.
And night and day
I will go forth to pray
  That she love me.

She is as gold
Lovely, and far more cold.
  Do thou pray with me,
For if I win grace
To kiss twice her face
  God has done well to me.

AT THE BRITISH MUSEUM

I TURN the page and read:
'I dream of silent verses where the rhyme
Glides noiseless as an oar.'

The heavy musty air, the black desks,
The bent heads and the rustling noises
In the great dome
Vanish . . .

And
The sun hangs in the cobalt-blue sky,
The boat drifts over the lake shallows,
The fishes swim like umber shades through the
    undulating weeds,
The oleanders drop their rosy petals on the lawns,
And the swallows dive and swirl and whistle
About the cleft battlements of Can Grande's
    castle. . . .

AT NIGHTS

AT nights I sit here,
Shading my eyes, shutting them if you glance up,
Pretending to doze,
And watching you,
Thinking . . .
I think of when I first saw the beauty of things—
God knows I was poor enough and sad enough
And humiliated enough—
But not all the slights and the poorness and the
    worry
Could hide away the green of the poplar leaves,
The ripples and light of the little stream,
The pattern of the ducks' feathers—
Like a Japanese print—
The dawns I saw in the winter
When I went shooting,
The summer walks and the winter walks,
The hot days with the cows coming down to the
    water,
The flowers,
Buttercups, meadowsweet, hog's parsley,
And the larks singing in the morning
And the thrushes singing at evening
When I went out in the fields, muttering poetry . . .
I looked at the world as God did
When first He made it.
I saw that it was good.
And now at nights,
Now that everything has gone right somehow,
And I have friends and books
And no more bitterness,
I sit here, shading my eyes,
Peeping at you, watching you,
Thinking.

CHURCH WALK, KENSINGTON

SUNDAY MORNING

THE cripples are going to church.
Their crutches beat upon the stones,
And they have clumsy iron boots.

Their clothes are black, their faces peaked and
   mean;
Their legs are withered
Like dried bean pods.
Their eyes are as stupid as frogs'.

And the god, September,
Has paused for a moment here
Garlanded with crimson leaves.
He held a branch of fruited oak.
He smiled like Hermes the beautiful
Cut in marble.

ST MARY'S, KENSINGTON

THE orange plane-leaves
Rest gently on the cracked grey slabs
In the city churchyard.

O pitiful dead,
There is not one of those who pass by
To remember you.

But the trees do not forget;
Their severed tresses
Are laid sadly above you.

EVENING

THE chimneys, rank on rank,
Cut the clear sky;
The moon
With a rag of gauze about her loins
Poses among them, an awkward Venus—

And here am I looking wantonly at her
Over the kitchen sink.

CINEMA EXIT

AFTER the click and whirr
Of the glimmering pictures,
The dry feeling in the eyes
As the sight follows the electric flickerings,
The banal sentimentality of the films,
The hushed concentration of the people,
The tinkling piano—
Suddenly,
A vast avalanche of greenish-yellow light
Pours over the threshold;
White globes darting vertical rays spot the
    sombre buildings;
The violent gloom of the night
Battles with the radiance;
Swift figures, legs, skirts, white cheeks, hats
Flicker in oblique rays of dark and light.

Millions of human vermin
Swarm sweating
Along the night-arched cavernous roads.

(Happily rapid chemical processes
Will disintegrate them all.)

IN THE TUBE

THE electric car jerks;
I stumble on the slats of the floor,
Fall into a leather seat
And look up.

A row of advertisements,
A row of windows,
Set in brown woodwork pitted with brass nails,
A row of hard faces,
Immobile,
In the swaying train,
Rush across the flickering background of fluted
    dingy tunnel;
A row of eyes,
Eyes of greed, of pitiful blankness, of plethoric
    complacency,
Immobile,
Gaze, stare at one point,
At my eyes.

Antagonism,
Disgust,
Immediate antipathy,
Cut my brain, as a dry sharp reed
Cuts a finger.
I surprise the same thought
In the brasslike eyes:
'*What right have you to live?*'

INTERLUDE

Blow your tin squeals
On your reedy whistle.

How they come
                        dancing,
White girls,
                        lithe girls,
In linked dance
From Attica.

Gay girls dancing
        in the frozen street,
Hair streaming, and white raiment
Flying,
Red lips that first were
Red in Ephesus.

Gone!
You? Red-nose, piping by the Red Lion,
You!
Did you bring them?

Here, take my pennies,
'*Mon semblable, mon frère!*'

HAMPSTEAD HEATH

EASTER MONDAY 1915

Dark clouds, torn into gaps of livid sky,
Pierced through
By a swift searchlight, a long white dagger.
The black murmuring crowd
Flows, eddies, stops, flows on
Between the lights
And the banks of noisy booths.

LONDON

MAY 1915

GLITTERING leaves
Dance in a squall;
Behind them bleak immoveable clouds.

A church spire
Holds up a little brass cock
To peck at the blue wheat fields.

Roofs, conical spires, tapering chimneys,
Livid with sunlight, lace the horizon.

A pear-tree, a broken white pyramid
In a dingy garden, troubles me
With ecstasy.

At night, the moon, a pregnant woman,
Walks cautiously over the slippery heavens.

And I am tormented,
Obsessed,
Among all this beauty,
With a vision of ruins,
Of walls crumbling into clay.

In an old dull yard near Camden Town,
Which echoes with the rattle of cars and 'buses
And freight-trains, puffing steam and smoke and
 dirt
To the steaming sooty sky—
There stands an old and grimy statue,
A statue of Psyche and her lover, Eros.

A little nearer Camden Town,
In a square of ugly sordid shops,
Is another statue, facing the Tube,
Staring with heavy purposeless glare
At the red and white shining tiles—
A tall stone statue of Cobden.
And though no one ever pauses to see
What hero it is that faces the Tube,
I can understand very well indeed
That England must honour its national heroes,
Must honour the hero of Free Trade—
Or was it the Corn Laws?—
That I can understand.

But what I shall never understand
Is the little group in the dingy yard
Under the dingier sky,
The Eros and Psyche—
Surrounded with pots and terra-cotta busts
And urns and broken pillars—
Eros, naked, with his wings stretched out
Just lighting down to kiss her on the lips.

What are they doing here in Camden Town
In the midst of all this clamour and filth?

They, who should stand in a sun-lit room
Hung with deep purple, painted with gods,
Paved with dark porphyry,
Stand for ever embraced
By the side of a rustling fountain
Over a marble basin
Carved with leopards and grapes and young men
    dancing;
Or in a garden leaning above Corinth,
Under the ilexes and the cypresses,
Very white against a very blue sky;
Or growing hoary, if they must grow old,
With lichens and softly creeping moss:
What are they doing here in Camden Town?
And who has brought their naked beauty
And their young fresh lust to Camden Town,
Which settled long ago to toil and sweat and
    filth,
Forgetting—to the greater glory of Free Trade—
Young beauty and young love and youthful
    flesh?

Slowly the rain settles down on them,
Slowly the soot eats into them,
Slowly the stone grows greyer and dirtier,
Till in spite of his spreading wings
Her eyes have a rim of soot
Half an inch deep,
And his wings, the tall god's wings,
That should be red and silver
Are ochreous brown.

And I peer from a 'bus-top
As we splash through the grease and puddles,
And I glimpse them, huddled against the wall,

Half-hidden under a freight-train's smoke,
And I see the limbs that a Greek slave cut
In some old Italian town,
I see them growing older
And sadder
And greyer.

1

THE bitterness, the misery, the wretchedness of child-
hood
Put me out of love with God,
I can't believe in God's goodness;
I can believe
In many avenging gods.
Most of all I believe
In gods of bitter dullness,
Cruel local gods
Who seared my childhood.

2

I've seen people put
A chrysalis in a match-box,
'To see,' they told me, 'what sort of moth would
come.'
But when it broke its shell
It slipped and stumbled and fell about its prison
And tried to climb to the light
For space to dry its wings.

That's how I was.
Somebody found my chrysalis
And shut it in a match-box.
My shrivelled wings were beaten,
Shed their colours in dusty scales
Before the box was opened
For the moth to fly.
And then it was too late,
Because the beauty a child has,
And the beautiful things it learns before its birth,
Were shed, like moth scales, from me.

I hate that town;
I hate the town I lived in when I was little;
I hate to think of it.
There were always clouds, smoke, rain
In that dingy little valley.
It rained; it always rained.
I think I never saw the sun until I was nine——
And then it was too late;
Everything's too late after the first seven years.

That long street we lived in
Was duller than a drain
And nearly as dingy.
There were the big College
And the pseudo-Gothic town-hall.
There were the sordid provincial shops—
The grocer's, and the shops for women,
The shop where I bought transfers,
And the piano and gramophone shop
Where I used to stand
Staring at the huge shiny pianos and at the pictures
Of a white dog staring into a gramophone.
How dull and greasy and grey and sordid it was.
On wet days—it was always wet—
I used to kneel on a chair
And look at it from the window.
The dirty yellow trams
Dragged noisily along
With a clatter of wheels and bells
And a humming of wires overhead.
They threw up the filthy rain-water from the hollow
    lines
And then the water ran back
Full of brownish foam bubbles.

There was nothing else to see—
It was all so dull—
Except a few grey legs under shiny black umbrellas
Running along the grey shiny pavements;
Sometimes there was a waggon
Whose horses made a strange loud hollow sound
With their hoofs
Through the silent rain.

And there was a grey museum
Full of dead birds and dead insects and dead animals
And a few relics of the Romans—dead also.
There was the sea-front,
A long asphalt walk with a bleak road beside it,
Three piers, a row of houses,
And a salt dirty smell from the little harbour.

I was like a moth—
Like one of those grey Emperor moths
Which flutter through the vines at Capri.
And that damned little town was my match-box,
Against whose sides I beat and beat
Until my wings were torn and faded, and dingy
As that damned little town.

4

At school it was just as dull as that dull High Street.
They taught me pothooks—
I wanted to be alone, although I was so little,
Alone, away from the rain, the dinginess, the dullness,
Away somewhere else—

The town was dull;
The front was dull;

The High Street and the other street were dull—
And there was a public park, I remember,
And that was damned dull, too,
With its beds of geraniums no one was allowed to
    pick,
And its clipped lawns you weren't allowed to walk on,
And the gold-fish pond you mustn't paddle in,
And the gate made out of a whale's jaw-bones,
And the swings, which were for 'Board-School
    children',
And its gravel paths.

And on Sundays they rang the bells
From Baptist and Evangelical and Catholic churches;
They had the Salvation Army.
I was taken to a High Church;
The parson's name was Mowbray,
'Which is a good name, but he thinks too much of
    it'—
That's what I heard people say.

I took a little black book
To that cold, grey, damp-smelling church,
And I had to sit on a hard bench,
Wriggle off it to stand up when they sang psalms—
And wriggle off it to kneel down when they prayed—
And then there was nothing to do
Except to play trains with the hymn-books.

There was nothing to see,
Nothing to do,
Nothing to play with,
Except that in a large empty room upstairs
There was a large tin box
Containing reproductions of the Magna Charta,

Of the Declaration of Independence,
And of a letter from Raleigh after the Armada.

There were also several packets of stamps,
Yellow and blue Guatemala parrots,
Blue stags and red baboons and birds from Sarawak,
Indians and Men-of-War
From the United States,
And the green and red portraits
Of King Francobollo
Of Italy.

5

I don't believe in God.
I do believe in avenging gods
Who plague us for sins we never sinned,
But who avenge us.
That's why I'll never have a child,
Never shut up a chrysalis in a match-box,
For the moth to spoil and crush its bright colours,
Beating its wings against the dingy prison-wall.

DAISY

You were my playmate by the sea—
We swam together
Your girl's body had no breasts.

We found prawns among the rocks;
We liked to feel the sun and to do nothing;
In the evening we played games with the others.

It made me glad to be by you.

Sometimes I kissed you,
And you were always glad to kiss me;
But I was afraid—I was only fourteen.

And I had quite forgotten you,
You and your name.

Today I pass through the streets,
She who touches my arm and talks with me
Is—who knows?—Helen of Sparta,
Dryope, Laodamia . . .

And there are you
A whore in Oxford Street.

WATER ruffled and speckled by galloping wind
Which puffs and spurts it into tiny pashing breakers
Dashed with lemon-yellow afternoon sunlight.
The shining of the sun upon the water
Is like a scattering of gold crocus petals
In a long wavering irregular flight.

The water is cold to the eye
As the wind to the cheek.

In the budding chestnuts
Whose sticky buds glimmer and are half burst open
The starlings make their clitter-clatter;
And the blackbirds in the grass
Are getting as fat as the pigeons.

Even the cold wind is seeking a new mistress.

NOISE;
Iron hoofs, iron wheels, iron din
Of drays and trams and feet passing;
Iron
Beaten to a vast mad cacophony.

*In vain the shrill far cry
Of swallows sweeping by;
In vain the silence and green
Of meadows Apriline;
In vain the clear white rain—*

Soot; mud;
A nation maddened with labour;
Interminable collision of energies—
Iron beating upon iron;
Smoke whirling upwards,
Speechless, impotent.

*In vain the shrill far cry
Of kittiwakes that fly
Where the sea waves leap green.
The meadows Apriline—*

Noise, iron, smoke;
Iron, iron, iron.

IMAGES

1

THROUGH the dark pine trunks
Silver and yellow gleam the clouds
And the sun;
The sea is faint purple.
My love, my love, I shall never reach you.

2

You are beautiful
As a straight red foxglove
Among green plants;
I stretched out my hand to caress you:
It is blistered by the envious nettles.

3

I have spent hours this morning
Seeking in the brook
For a clear pebble
To remind me of your eyes.

And all the sleepless hours of night
I think of you.

4

Your kisses are poignant,
Ah! why must I leave you?

Here alone I scribble and re-scribble
The words of a long-dead Greek poet:
'*Love, thou art terrible,*
Ah, Love, thou art bitter-sweet!'

LET the sea beat its thin torn hands
In anguish against the shore,
Let it moan
Between headland and cliff;
Let the sea shriek out its agony
Across waste sands and marshes,
And clutch great ships,
Tearing them plate from steel plate
In reckless anger;
Let it break the white bulwarks
Of harbour and city;
Let it sob and scream and laugh
In a sharp fury,
With white salt tears
Wet on its writhen face;
Ah! let the sea still be mad
And crash in madness among the shaking rocks—
For the sea is the cry of sorrow.

THE limbs of gods,
Still, veined marble,
Rest heavily in sleep
Under a saffron twilight.

Not for them battle,
Severed limbs, death, and a cry of victory;
Not for them strife
And a torment of storm.

A vast breast moves slowly,
The great thighs shift,
The stone eyelids rise;
The slow tongue speaks:

'*Only a rain of bright dust*
In the outer air;
A little whisper of wind;
Sleep; rest; forget.'

Bright dust of battle!
A little whisper of dead souls!

VAGABONDS of beauty,
Wistful, exquisite waifs
From a lost, and a forgotten, and a lovely land,
We cannot comfort you
Though our souls yearn for you.

You are delicate strangers
In a gloomy town,
Stared at and hated—
Gold crocus blossoms in a drab lane.

We cannot comfort you;
Your life is anguish;
All we can do—
Mutely bring pungent herbs and branches of oak
And resinous scented pine wreaths
To hide the crown of thorny pain
Crushing your white frail foreheads.

PRAYER

I AM a garden of red tulips
And late daffodils and bay-hedges,
A small sunk garden
About an oblong pool
With three grey lead Dutch tanks—
I am this garden shattered and blown
With a day-long western gale
And bursts of rapid rain.

There are dank petals in the ruffled waters,
And muddy flowers upon the path.
The grass is covered with torn leaves.

God of gardens, dear small god of gardens,
Grant me faint glow of sunlight,
A last bird hopping in the quiet haze,
Then let the night swoop swiftly,
Fold round and crush out life
For ever.

CAPTIVE

THEY have torn the gold tettinx
From my hair;
And wrenched the bronze sandals
From my ankles.

They have taken from me my friend
Who knew the holy wisdom of poets,
Who had drunk at the feast
Where Simonides sang.

No more do I walk the calm gardens
In the white mist of olives;
No more do I take the rose-crown
From the white hands of a maiden.

I, who was free, am a slave;
The Muses have forgotten me,
The gods do not hear me.

Here there are no flowers to love;
But afar off I dream that I see
Bent poppies and the deathless asphodel.

SUNSETS

THE white body of the evening
Is torn into scarlet,
Slashed and gouged and seared
Into crimson,
And hung ironically
With garlands of mist.

And the wind
Blowing over London from Flanders
Has a bitter taste.

A GOD's strength lies
More in the fervour of his worshippers
Than in his own divinity.
Who now regards me or who twines
Red wool and threaded lilies round the brows
Of my neglected statues?
Who now seeks my aid
To add skill to the hunter's hand
Or save some pregnant ewe or bitch
Helpless in travail?
None, since that fierce autumn noon
I lay asleep under Zeus-holy oaks
Heavy with syrupy wine and tired
With the close embraces
Of some sweet wearer of the leopard-skin—
That noon they snared and bound me as I slept
And dragged me for their uncouth mirth
Out of my immemorial woods and crags
Down to their bastard hamlets.

Then the god's blood my father spilled
To get me upon a mortal stock, dwindled and
    shrank,
And I was impotent and weak
As the once desirable flesh of my human mother;
I that should have been dreaded in wan recesses,
Worshipped in high woods, a striker of terror
To the wayfarer in lonely places,
I, a lord of golden flesh and dim music,
I, a captive and coarsely derided!
Ai! I could bite the brown flesh
Of my arms and hands for shame and grief.

I am weary for the freedom of free things,
The old gay life of the half-god,
Who had no dread of death or sorrow.
I am weary for the open spaces,
The long damp sands acrid with many tides,
And the infinite wistfulness of evening seas.
I am weary for wooded silences,
The nymph-rapt hours of heat,
The slow cool lapse of moonlit nights,
The solitude of the mysterious stars
Pearlwise scattered upon the domed breast of the
    Great Mother,
Oh, weary for my brown clean streams,
And wet petals of woodland flowers,
Scented with dew and delicate as a kiss.

Here they grow careless, thinking me a coward,
But one night I shall break these thongs
And kill, kill, kill in sharp revenge.
Then out of doors by the lush pastures
To the heath and the foot-hills and the hills,
To the wild-rose kisses of the deathless girls
Who laugh and flash among the trees,
Out to the unploughed lands no foot oppresses,
The lands that are free, being free of man.

IMAGES OF WAR

PROEM

Out of this turmoil and passion,
This implacable contest,
This vast sea of effort,
I would gather something of repose,
Some intuition of the inalterable gods.

Each day I grow more restless,
See the austere shape elude me,
Gaze impotently upon a thousand miseries
And still am dumb.

VICARIOUS ATONEMENT

THIS is an old and very cruel god. . . .

We will endure;
We will try not to wince
When he crushes and rends us.

If indeed it is for your sakes,
If we perish or moan in torture,
Or stagger under sordid burdens
That you may live—
Then we can endure.

If our wasted blood
Make bright the page
Of poets yet to be;
If this our tortured life
Save from destruction's nails
Gold words of a Greek long dead;
Then we can endure,
Then hope,
Then watch the sun rise
Without utter bitterness.

But, O thou old and very cruel god,
Take, if thou will, this bitter cup from us.

LEAVE-TAKING

WILL the world still live for you
When I am gone?

Will the straight garden poppy
Still spout blood from its green throat
Before your feet?
Will the five cleft petals of the campion
Still be rose-coloured,
Like five murdered senses, for you?

Will your trees still live,
Thrust metallic bosses of leafage
From the hillside in the summer light;
Will the leaves sway and grow darker,
Rustle, swirl in the gales;
Decay into gold and orange,
Crinkle and shrivel,
And fall silently at last
On to frosty grass?

Will there be sun for you;
The line of near hills
Cut as in thin blue steel
Against red haze?

Will there be silence?

Will not even the clean acrid sea
Turn stale upon your lips?

Will the world die for you
As it dies for me?

BONDAGE

I HAVE been a spendthrift—
Dropping from lazy fingers
Quiet coloured hours,
Fluttering away from me
Like oak and beech leaves in October.

I have lived keenly and wastefully,
Like a bush or a sun insect—
Lived sensually and thoughtfully,
Loving the flesh and the beauty of this world—
Green ivy about ruined towers,
The outpouring of the grey sea,
And the ecstasy
Of a pale clear sky at sunset.

I have been prodigal of love
For cities and for lonely places;
I have tried not to hate mankind;
I have gathered sensations
Like ripe fruits in a rich orchard. . . .
All this is gone;
There are no leaves, no sea,
No shade of a rich orchard,
Only a sterile, dusty waste,
Empty and threatening.
I long vainly for solitude,
And the lapse of silent hours;
I am frantic to throw off
My heavy cloth and leather garments,
To set free my feet and body.
And I am so far from beauty
That a yellow daisy seems to clutch my heart
With eager searching petals,
And I am grateful even to humility
For the taste of pure clean bread.

FIELD MANOEUVRES

OUTPOST DUTY

THE long autumn grass under my body
Soaks my clothes with its dew;
Where my knees press into the ground
I can feel the damp earth.

In my nostrils is the smell of the crushed grass,
Wet pine-cones and bark.

Through the great bronze pine trunks
Glitters a silver segment of road.
Interminable squadrons of silver and blue horses
Pace in long ranks the blank fields of heaven.

There is no sound;
The wind hisses gently through the pine needles;
The flutter of a finch's wings about my head
Is like distant thunder,
And the shrill cry of a mosquito
Sounds loud and close.

I am 'to fire at the enemy column
After it has passed'—
But my obsolete rifle, loaded with 'blank',
Lies untouched before me,
My spirit follows after the gliding clouds,
And my lips murmur of the mother of beauty
Standing breast-high, in golden broom
Among the blue pine-woods!

DAWN

THE grim dawn lightens thin bleak clouds;
In the hills beyond the flooded meadows
Lies death-pale, death-still mist.

We trudge along wearily,
Heavy with lack of sleep,
Spiritless, yet with pretence of gaiety.

The sun brings crimson to the colourless sky;
Light shines from brass and steel;
We trudge on wearily—
Our unspoken prayer:
'God, end this black and aching anguish
Soon, with vivid crimson agonies of death,
End it in mist-pale sleep.'

THE LOVER

THOUGH I have had friends
And a beautiful love
There is one lover I await above all.

She will not come to me
In the time of soft plum-blossoms
When the air is gay with birds singing
And the sky is a delicate caress;
She will come
From the midst of a vast clamour
With a mist of stars about her
And great beckoning plumes of smoke
Upon her leaping horses.

And she will bend suddenly and clasp me;
She will clutch me with fierce arms
And stab me with a kiss like a wound
That bleeds slowly.

But though she will hurt me at first
In her strong gladness
She will soon soothe me gently
And cast upon me an unbreakable sleep
Softly for ever.

A MOMENT'S INTERLUDE

ONE night I wandered alone from my comrades'
    huts;
The grasshoppers chirped softly
In the warm misty evening;
Bracken fronds beckoned from the darkness
With exquisite frail green fingers;
The tree-gods muttered affectionately about me
And from the distance came the grumble of a
    kindly train.

I was so happy to be alone
So full of love for the great speechless earth,
That I could have laid my cheek in the grasses
And caressed with my lips the hard sinewy body
Of Earth, the cherishing mistress of bitter lovers.

INSOUCIANCE

IN and out of the dreary trenches
Trudging cheerily under the stars
I make for myself little poems
Delicate as a flock of doves.

They fly away like white-winged doves.

ON THE MARCH

BRIGHT berries on the roadside,
Clear among your dusty leaves,
Red mottled berries,
You are beautiful
As the points of a girl's breasts;
You are as firm and fresh.

Beauty of the morning sun
Among the red berries
Of early September,
You tear at my breast,
Your light crushes me
With memory of freedom lost
And warm hours blotted out.

I will throw away rifle and leather belt,
Straps, khaki and heavy nailed boots,
And run naked across the dewy grass
Among the firm red berries!
I will be free
And sing of beauty and the women of Hellas,
Of rent seas and the peace of olive gardens,
Of these rough meadows,
Of the keen welcome smell of London mud!
I will be free. . . .

Party—HALT!

IN THE TRENCHES

1

Not that we are weary,
Not that we fear,
Not that we are lonely
Though never alone—
Not these, not these destroy us;
But that each rush and crash
Of mortar and shell,
Each cruel bitter shriek of bullet
That tears the wind like a blade,
Each wound on the breast of earth,
Of Demeter, our Mother,
Wound us also,
Sever and rend the fine fabric
Of the wings of our frail souls,
Scatter into dust the bright wings
Of Psyche!

2

Impotent,
How impotent is all this clamour,
This destruction and contest. . . .
Night after night comes the moon
Haughty and perfect;
Night after night the Pleiades sing
And Orion swings his belt across the sky.
Night after night the frost
Crumbles the hard earth.

Soon the spring will drop flowers
And patient creeping stalk and leaf
Along these barren lines
Where the huge rats scuttle
And the hawk shrieks to the carrion crow.

Can you stay them with your noise?
Then kill winter with your cannon,
Hold back Orion with your bayonets
And crush the spring leaf with your armies!

ANANKE

In bitter sorrow and despair
I said unto my love:
'All the far meadows, the cool marsh
And scented uplands I have searched
For blossoms pleasant to the gods;
I have begged just ripened fruits
From all the pitying tree-nymphs,
Have gathered many honey-combs,
Poured wine,
Poured milk,
Poured all my words, in vain—
For yet the implacable gods
Turn their untroubled faces
Austerely from me,
Yet the cold envious wind
Whispers that no man born
Tricks the wide-open eyes of Fate'.

And seeing the pallor of her cheek,
Her fear-tormented eyes and tremulous hands,
I turned aside
To check the desperate tears burning my eyes;
Then came to her again, smiling,
And kissed her lips,
Saying no word save this:
'Do not despair'.

But yet
I have not seen her since that day.

MISERY

SOMETIMES in bitter mood I mock myself:
'Half ape, half ass, servant and slave,
Where are your dreams gone now,
Where your fierce pride?
Whither goes your youth?
And how will you dare touch again
Dear slender women with those disfigured hands?
Or bare your long-dishonoured body
To the contemptuous sun?
How live after this shame?'

And all my answer:
'So that hate poison not my days,
And I still love the earth,
Flowers and all living things,
And my song still be keen and clear
I can endure.'

LIVING SEPULCHRES

ONE frosty night when the guns were still
I leaned against the trench
Making for myself *hokku*
Of the moon and flowers and of the snow.

But the ghostly scurrying of huge rats
Swollen with feeding upon men's flesh
Filled me with shrinking dread.

DAUGHTER OF ZEUS

Tuerons la lune [Marinetti]

No!
We will not slay the moon.
For she is the fairest of the daughters of Zeus,
Of the maidens of Olympus.

And though she be pale and yet more pale
Gazing upon dead men
And fierce disastrous strife,
Yet for us she is still a frail lily
Floating upon a calm pool—
Still a tall lady comforting our human despair.

PICKET

Dusk and deep silence . . .

Three soldiers huddled on a bench
Over a red-hot brazier,
And a fourth who stands apart
Watching the cold rainy dawn.

Then the familiar sound of birds—
Clear cock-crow, caw of rooks,
Frail pipe of linnet, the 'ting! ting!' of
  chaffinches,
And over all the lark
Outpiercing even the robin . . .

Wearily the sentry moves
Muttering the one word: 'Peace'.

TRENCH IDYLL

We sat together in the trench,
He on a lump of frozen earth
Blown in the night before,
I on an unexploded shell;
And smoked and talked, like exiles,
Of how pleasant London was,
Its women, restaurants, night clubs, theatres,
How at that very hour
The taxi-cabs were taking folk to dine. . . .
Then we sat silent for a while
As a machine-gun swept the parapet.

He said:
'I've been here on and off two years
And seen only one man killed'.

'That's odd.'

'The bullet hit him in the throat;
He fell in a heap on the fire-step,
And called out "My God! *dead!*" '

'Good Lord, how terrible!'

'Well, as to that, the nastiest job I've had
Was last year on this very front
Taking the discs at night from men
Who'd hung for six months on the wire
Just over there.
The worst of all was
They fell to pieces at a touch.
Thank God we couldn't see their faces;
They had gas helmets on . . .'

I shivered;
'It's rather cold here, sir, suppose we move?'

TIME'S CHANGES

Four years ago today in Italy
I gathered wild flowers for a girl—
Thick scented broom, wild sword-flowers,
The red anemones that line the ways
And the frail-throated freesia
Which lives beneath the orange boughs
And whose faint scent to me
Is love's own breath, its kiss. . . .

Today in sunless barren fields
I gather heads of shells,
Splinters of shrapnel, cartridges. . . .

What shall I gather
Four years from today?

A VILLAGE

1

Now if you saw my village
You'd not think it beautiful,
But flat and commonplace—
As I'd have called it half a year ago. . . .

2

But when you've pondered
Hour upon chilly hour in those damned
    trenches
You get at the significance of things,
Get to know, clearer than before,
What a tree means, what a pool,
Or a black wet field in sunlight.

You get to know,
In that shell-pierced silence,
Under the unmoved ironic stars,
How good love of the earth is.

So I go strolling,
Hands deep in pockets, head aslant,
And eyes screwed up against the light,
Just loving things
Like any other lunatic or lover.

3

For there's so much to love,
So much to see and understand,
So much naïvéte, whimsicality,
Even in a dull village like this.

Pigeons and fowls upon a pointed haystack;
The red-tiled barns we sleep in;
The profile of the distant town
Misty against the leaden-silver sky;

Two ragged willows and a fallen elm
With an end of broken wall
Glimmering through evening mist—
All worthy Rembrandt's hand,
Rembrandt who loved homely things. . . .

Then there's the rain pool where we wash,
Skimming the film-ice with our tingling
    hands;
The elm-fringed dykes and solemn placid
    fields
Flat as a slate and blacker.
There's the church—
The poorest ever built, I think—
With all its painted plaster saints
Straight from the Rue St Sulpice,
Its dreadful painted windows,
And Renaissance 'St Jacques le Majeur'
Over the porch. . . .

4

Today the larks are up,
The willow boughs are red with sap,
The last ice melting on the dykes;
One side there stands a row of poplars,
Slender amazons, martial and tall,
And on the other
The sunlight makes the red-tiled roofs deep
    orange. . . .

5

And we have come from death,
From the long weary nights and days
Out in those frozen wire-fringed ditches;
And this is life again, rich life—
This poor drab village, lovely in our eyes
As the prince city of Tuscany
Or the crown of Asia, Damascus.

THE WINE CUP

LIFE was to us an amphora of wine
Pressed from full grapes
Upon the warm slopes of the Cyclades—
Wine that brings light
Into the gloomiest eyes of man,
Wine, cooled and mingled for the eager lip.

We had but gazed upon the amphora,
Touching the figures painted on its flanks—
Achilles reining in his four great horses
Or Maenads dancing to a Faun's pipe.

We had but sipped the wine,
Watching its changing hue—
Deep purple in the shadowy amphora
But crimson where the light
Pierces the crystal cup.

And if we thought:
'True, the cup soon is emptied,
The amphora rings hollow
And our veins lack warmth and life'—
It did but give a gentle melancholy
Making our present joy more keen and clear.

But now
Cold, terrible, unseen hands
Have dragged the cup from us.
We are distracted
As a poor goatherd of the Thracian hills
Robbed of his flock and sun-tanned wife
Hurrying in anguish to the unfriendly town
As we to death.

MACHINE GUNS

GOLD flashes in the dark,
And on the road
Each side, behind, in front of us,
Gold sparks
Where the fierce bullets strike the stones.

In a near shell-hole lies a wounded man,
The stretcher-bearers bending over him;
And at our feet
Cower shrinkingly against the ground
Dark shadowy forms of men.

Only we two stand upright;
All differences of life and character smoothed
   out
And nothing left
Save that one foolish tie of caste
That will not let us shrink.

BATTLEFIELD

THE wind is piercing chill
And blows fine grains of snow
Over this shell-rent ground;
Every house in sight
Is smashed and desolate.

But in this fruitless land,
Thorny with wire
And foul with rotting clothes and sacks,
The crosses flourish—
Ci-gît, ci-gît, ci-gît . . .
'Ci-gît 1 soldat Allemand,
Priez pour lui.'

THREE LITTLE GIRLS

MARIANNE, Madeline, Alys,
Three little girls I used to see
Two months ago,
Three little girls with fathers killed
And mothers lost,
Three little girls with broken shoes
And hard sharp coughs,
Three little girls who sold us sweets
Too near the shells,
Three little girls with names of saints
And angels' eyes,
Three little girls, where are you now?
Marianne, Madeline, Alys.

A RUINED HOUSE

THOSE who lived here are gone
Or dead or desolate with grief;
Of all their life here nothing remains
Except their trampled, dirtied clothes
Among the dusty bricks,
Their marriage bed, rusty and bent,
Thrown down aside as useless;
And a broken toy left by their child. . . .

No, I'm not afraid of death
(Not very much afraid, that is)
Either for others or myself;
Can watch them coming from the line
On the wheeled silent stretchers
And not shrink,
But munch my sandwich stoically
And make a joke, when 'it' has passed.

But—the way they wobble!—
God! that makes one sick.
Dead men should be so still, austere,
And beautiful,
Not wobbling carrion roped upon a cart . . .

Well, thank God for rum.

I WAS wrong, quite wrong;
The dead men are not always carrion.
After the advance,
As we went through the shattered trenches
Which the enemy had left,
We found, lying upon the fire-step,
A dead English soldier,
His head bloodily bandaged
And his closed left hand touching the earth,

More beautiful than one can tell,
More subtly coloured than a perfect Goya,
And more austere and lovely in repose
Than Angelo's hand could ever carve in stone.

A YOUNG TREE

THERE are so few trees here, so few young trees,
That Fate might have been merciful
And turned aside the shock of flame
That strewed your branches on the turned-up earth,
Ending the joy we had in your fresh leaves.

And every keen dear lad that's killed
Seems to cry out:
'We are so few, so very few,
Could not our fate have been more merciful?'

REVERIE

IT is very hot in the chalk trench
With its rusty iron pickets
And shell-smashed crumbling traverses,
Very hot and choking and full of evil smells
So that my head and eyes ache
And I am glad to crawl away
And lie in the little shed I call mine.
And because I want to be alone
They keep coming to me and asking:
'How many billets have we in such a trench?'
Or, 'Do you know the way to such a redoubt?'

But these things pass over, beyond and away
      from me,
The voices of the men fade into silence
For I am burned with a sweet madness,
Soothed also by the fire that burns me,
Exalted and made happy in misery
By love, by an unfaltering love.
If I could tell you of this love—
But I can tell only lovers,
Only irresponsible imprudent lovers
Who give and have given and will give
All for love's sake,
All just to kiss her hand, her frail hand.

I will not tell you how long it is
Since I kissed and touched her hand
And was happy looking at her,
Yet every day and every night
She seems to be with me, beside me,
And there is great love between us
Although we are so far apart.

And although the hot sun burns in the white
    trench
And the shells go shrilling overhead
And I am harassed by stupid questions,
I do not forget her,
I do not forget to build dreams of her
That are only less beautiful than she is.

For there are some who love God,
And some their country and some gain,
Some are happy to exact obedience
And some to obey for the sake of a cause—
But I am indifferent to all these things
Since it was for her sake only I was born
So that I should love her.

Perhaps I shall be killed and never see her again,
Perhaps it will be but a wreck of me that returns
    to her,
Perhaps I shall kiss her hand once more,
But I am quite happy about Fate,
For this is love's beauty
That it does not die with lovers
But lives on, like a flower born from a god's
    blood,
Long after the lovers are dead.

Reason has pleaded in my brain
And Despair has whispered in my heart
That we die and vanish utterly;
I have seen dead men lying on the earth
Or carried slowly in stretchers,
And the chilled blood leaped in my heart
Saying: 'This is the end, there is no escape'.

But for love's sake I brush all this away
For, since I do not know why love is
Nor whence it comes, nor for what end,
It may very well be that I am wrong about
    death,
And that among the dead also there are lovers.

Would that we were dead, we two,
Dead centuries upon centuries,
Forgotten, even our race and tongue forgotten,
Would that we had been dead so long
That no memory of this fret of life
Could ever trouble us.

We would be together, always together
Always in a land of many flowers,
And bright sunlight and cool shade;
We should not even need to kiss
Or join our hands;
It would be enough to be together.

She would stoop and gather a flower,
A pale, sweet-scented, fragile flower
(A flower whose name I will not tell,
The symbol of all love to us).

And I would watch her smile
And see the fair flowers of her breast
As the soft-coloured garment opened from her
    throat.

I would not speak, I would not speak one word
Though many ages of the world's time passed—
She would be bending by the flower's face
And I would stand beside and look and love.

Not far away as I now write
The guns are beating madly upon the still air
With sudden rapid blows of sound,
And men die with the quiet sun above them
And horror and pain and noise upon earth.

Tomorrow, maybe, I shall be one of them,
One in a vast field of dead men,
Unburied, or buried hastily, callously.
But for ever and for ever
In the fair land I have built up
From the dreams of my love,
We two are together, she bending by the pale
    flower
And I beside her:
We two together in a land of quiet
Inviolable behind the walls of death.

APRIL LIEDER

WHEN I rose up this morning
In a ruined town of France,
I heard the sparrows twitter
In gardens bare and grey
And watched the sunbeams dance.

O glad young April day!

When I lie down this evening
In a damp cellar of France
I'll hear the big guns booming
By bare and blasted lanes,
And watch the shrapnel dance.

O wild sad April rains!

BARRAGE

THUNDER,
The gallop of innumerable Valkyrie impetuous for
    battle,
The beating of vast eagle wings above Prometheus,
The contest of tall barbaric gods smitten by the
    hammer of Thor,
Pursuit! Pursuit! Pursuit!
The huge black dogs of hell
Leaping full-mouthed in murderous pursuit!

AN EARTH GODDESS

You are not the august Mother
Nor even one of her comely daughters,
But you gave shelter to men,
Hid birds and little beasts within your hands
And twined flowers in your hair.

Sister, you have been sick of a long fever,
You have been torn with throes
Fiercer than childbirth and yet barren;
You are plague-marked;
There are now no flowers in your hair.

I have seen your anguish, O Sister,
I have seen your wounds.
But now there is come upon you peace,
A peace unbroken, profound,
Such as came upon the mother of King Eteocles
When both her sons were dead.
For in your agony, Sister,
When men bruised and ravished you,
You remembered the wide kindness of our Mother
And gave shelter to each of them that rent you,
Shielded them from death with your delicate body
And received their clotted corpses into your once
    pure breast.

And now since you endured,
Since for all your wrong and bitter pain
There came no hatred upon you
But only pity and anguish
Such as the mother of King Eteocles felt
Gazing upon her two angry sons—
Because of this, your peace is wonderful.

Underfoot are a few scant grasses
Amid rusty ruin;
Overhead the last of your larks
Cries shrilly before the broken clouds;
But for your sake, O my Sister,
O daughter of our great Earth-Mother,
Because of your old pain
And long-suffering and sweetness,
Because of the new peace
Which lies so deeply upon you,
The chains of my bitterness are broken,
The weight of my despair leaves me.

BOMBARDMENT

Four days the earth was rent and torn
By bursting steel,
The houses fell about us;
Three nights we dared not sleep,
Sweating, and listening for the imminent crash
Which meant our death.

The fourth night every man,
Nerve-tortured, racked to exhaustion,
Slept, muttering and twitching,
While the shells crashed overhead.

The fifth day there came a hush;
We left our holes
And looked above the wreckage of the earth
To where the white clouds moved in silent lines
Across the untroubled blue.

EPITAPH

1

You are dead——
You, the kindly, courteous,
You whom we loved,
You who harmed no man
Yet were brave to death
And died that other men might live.

Far purer, braver lips than mine should praise
    you,
Far nobler hands than mine record your loss,
Yet since your courteous high valour scorned no
    man,
I, who but loved you from the ranks, can greet
    you,
Salute your grave and murmur: 'Brother,
Hail and farewell'.

EPITAPH

2

E.T. KILLED MAY 1917

You too are dead,
The coarse and ignorant,
Carping against all that was too high
For your poor spirit to grasp,
Cruel and evil-tongued—
Yet you died without a moan or whimper.

Oh, not I, not I should dare to judge you!
But rather leave with tears your grave
Where the sweet grass will cover all your faults
And all your courage too.

Brother, hail and farewell.

CONCERT

THESE antique prostitutions—
I deplore my own vague cynicism,
Undressing with indifferent eyes each girl,
Seeing them naked on that paltry stage
Stared at by half a thousand lustful eyes.

These antique prostitutions—
Am I dead? Withered? Grown old?
That not the least flush of desire
Tinges my unmoved flesh,
And that instead of women's living bodies
I see dead men—you understand?—dead men
With sullen, dark red gashes
Luminous in a foul trench?

These antique prostitutions.

TAINTIGNIES

BELGIUM

THIS land is tedious as a worn-out whore;
Faded and shabby
As her once bright face
Grown tarnished with disease,
Loathsome as her grin which shows
The black cubes of the missing teeth;
The very sky is drab and sear
As her lifeless hair,
The earth itself rotten and foul
As her dishonoured flesh.

TERROR

1

THOSE of the earth envy us,
Envy our beauty and frail strength,
Those of the wind and the moon
Envy our pain.

2

For as doe that has never borne child
We were swift to fly from terror;
And as fragile edged steel
We turned, we pierced, we endured.

3

We have known terror;
The terror of the wind and silent shadows,
The terror of great heights,
The terror of the worm,
The terror of thunder and fire,
The terror of water and slime,
The terror of horror and fear,
The terror of desire and pain—
The terror of apathy.

4

As a beast, as an arrow of pine,
Terror cleft us,
Tore us in envy away,
So that for month upon month
Pain wore us, hope left us, despair clutched us,
For they of the earth envied us,
Envied our beauty and strength.

5

Yet because, though we faltered and wept,
We held fast, clung close to our love,
Scorned hate even as they scorned us,
Some god has lightened our lives
Given back the cool mouth of song,
The mouth crushed like a flower.

6

We have suffered, we have bled,
And those of the wind and the moon
Envy our pain, the pain of the terror,
The delight no terror could slay.

DEFEAT

THOUGH our hearts were mad and strong
With love for you,
Though we fought for you,
Though our remnant struggled
And not one was false,
We are beaten.

Beauty, for your sake we are lost,
For you we are crushed,
Scorn and bitterness are cast at us,
And fools who hate you
Are preferred to us.

Treacherous wonderful lady,
You have betrayed us—
Yet, hurt and overwhelmed and in despair
We can but turn to you again
And sing our love for you.

White goddess of beauty,
Take these roses—
It is our blood that colours them;
Take these lilies—
White as our intense hearts;
Take these wind-flowers—
Frail as our strength spent in your service;
Take these hyacinths—
Graven with the sigh of our lost days;
Take these narcissus blooms
Lovely as your naked breasts.

White goddess of beauty,
Though the stars rose against you
And the steeds of the day

Were arrayed against you,
Though the might of the sea
And the menace of night
Were against you,
We would be with you
And worship you.

Ah, goddess! Lovely, implacable,
What wine shall we bring,
What cup for your lips?
Blood, blood of our hearts for a drink,
Our lives for a cup.

White grape and red grape and pale
Dim scarlet of wearied mouths,
Flowers and the music of trees,
Hills golden with sun
And the sea, still and blue and divine—
These are yours
But not ours.

We are scorned for your sake,
We are broken,
Ah, goddess! You turn from our pain!

And once we begged of you death,
Death, quiet and smiling,
Death cold as the wind of the sea.

Now, love has lighted our hearts,
Now, though we are beaten and crushed,
Grant us life.

Grant us life to suffer for you,
To feed your delicate lips,

With the strength of our blood,
To crown you with flowers of our pain
And hail you with cries of our woe,
Yet sweet and divine.

Grant us life!
If we die there is none upon earth
To feed the fierce pride of your heart;
There is none so fine and so keen,
There is none to sing at your feast.

Grant us life,
And gold lyre and box-wood pipe
Shall sound from hill-top and shore,
From the depth of the city street,
From under the horror of battle,
Faint as we faint in despair,
Yet clear in your praise.

We dream of white crags,
Skies changing and swift,
Of rain upon earth,
Of flowers soft as your fingers
And bright as your garments of love.

We have none of these things;
Only strife and despair and pain,
Lands hideous and days disfigured,
A grey sea and a muddy shore.
But for you we forget all this,
We forget our defeat,
All, all, for your sake.

DOUBT

1

CAN we, by any strength of ours
Thrust back this hostile world
That tears us from ourselves,
As a child from the womb,
A weak lover from light breasts?

Is there any hope?
Can we believe
That not in wild perversity,
In blinding cruelty,
Has flesh torn flesh,
Has soul been torn from soul?

Must we despair?
Throw back upon the gods this taunt
That even their loveliest is at best
Some ineffectual lie?

2

Sand in the gale whirls up,
Pricks and stifles our flesh,
Blinds and deafens our sense
So that we cannot hear
The crumbling downfall of the waves
Nor see the limpid sunlight any more.

But could we thrust from us
This threat, this misery,
Borrow the mountain's strength
As now its loneliness,
Hurl back this menace on itself,
Crush bronze with bronze—

Why, it would be as if some tall slim god
Unburdened of his age-long apathy,
Took in his hand the thin horn of the moon
And set it to his lips
And blew sharp wild shrill notes
Such as our hearts, our lonely hearts,
Have yearned for in the dumb bleak silences.

3

Ah! Weak as wax against their bronze are we,
Ah! Faint as reed-pipes by the water's roar,
And driven as land-birds by the vast sea wind.

RESENTMENT

WHY should you try to crush me?
Am I so Christ-like?

You beat against me,
Immense waves, filthy with refuse.
I am the last upright of a smashed breakwater
But you shall not crush me
Though you bury me in foaming slime
And hiss your hatred about me.

You break over me, cover me;
I shudder at the contact;
Yet I pierce through you
And stand up, torn, dripping, shaken,
But whole and fierce.

DISDAIN

HAVE the gods then left us in our need
Like base and common men?
Were even the sweet grey eyes
Of Artemis a lie,
The speech of Hermes but a trick,
The glory of Apollonian hair deceit?

Desolate we move across a desolate land,
The high gates closed,
No answer to our prayer;
Naught left save our integrity,
No murmur against Fate
Save that we are juster than the unjust gods,
More pitiful than they.

APATHY

COME down the road and do not speak.
You cannot know how strange it is
To walk upon a grey firm road again,
To feel the noiseless waves of air break on one's flesh.

You do not speak, you do not look at me;
Just walk in silence on the grey firm road
Guessing my mood by instinct, not by thought—
For there is no weapon of tongue or glance
So keen that it can stir my apathy,
Can stab that bitterness to hope,
Can pierce that humour to despair.

Silence fits the mood then—silence and you.

The trees beside the road—can you interpret
These fragments of leaf-music,
Here a phrase, and here a sort of melody
That dies to silence or is broken
By a full rustling that is discord?
Can you interpret such a simple thing?

Can I interpret this blank apathy,
This humorous bitterness?
Lean on the bridge now—do not speak—
And watch the coloured water slipping past,
While I struggle with myself,
Confront half-impulses, half-desires,
Grapple with lustreless definitions,
Grin at my inarticulate impotence
And so fall back on—apathy!

The bridge has three curved spans,
Is made of weathered stones,

And rests upon two diamond-pointed piers—
Is picturesque.
(I have not lost all touch and taste for life,
See beauty just as keenly, relish things.)
The water here is black and specked with white;
Under that tree the shallows grow to brown,
Light amber where the sunlight struggles
    through—
And yet what colour is it if you watch the reeds
Or if you only see the trees' reflection?

Flat on the surface rest the lily leaves
(Some curled up inwards, though, like boats)
And yellow heads thrust up on fine green throats.
Two—three—a dozen—watch now—demoiselle flies
Flicker and flutter and dip and rest
Their beryl-green or blue, dark Prussian blue,
    frail wings
On spits and threads of water-plant.
Notice all carefully, be precise, welcome the
    world.
Do I miss these things? Overlook beauty?
Not even the shadow of a bird
Passing across that white reflected cloud.

And yet there's always something else—
The way one corpse held its stiff yellow fingers
And pointed, pointed to the huge dark hole
Gouged between ear and jaw right to the skull.

Did I startle you? What was the matter?
Just a joke they told me yesterday,
Really, really, not for ladies' ears.
Forgive me; I'll not laugh so suddenly again.

THE BLOOD OF THE YOUNG MEN

1

Give us back the close veil of the senses,
Let us not see, ah, hide from us
The red blood splashed upon the walls,
The good red blood, the young, the lovely blood
Trampled unseeingly by passing feet,
Feet of the old men, feet of the cold cruel women,
Feet of the careless children, endlessly passing. . . .

2

Day has become an agony, night alone now,
That leisurely shadow, hides the blood-stains,
The horrible stains and clots of day-time.

3

All the garments of all the people,
All the wheels of all the traffic,
All the cold indifferent faces,
All the fronts of the houses,
All the stones of the street—
Ghastly! Horribly smeared with blood-stains.

4

The horror of it!
When a woman holds out a white hand
Suddenly to know it drips black putrid blood;
When an old man sits, serene and healthy,
In clean white linen, with clean white hair,
Suddenly to know the linen foully spotted,
To see the white hair streaked with dripping blood.

5

O these pools and ponds of blood,
Slowly dripped in, slowly brimming lakes,

Blood of the young men, blood of their bodies,
Squeezed and crushed out to purple the garments of
    Dives,
Poured out to colour the lips of Magdalen,
Magdalen who loves not, whose sins are loveless.
O this steady drain of the weary bodies,
This beating of hearts growing dimmer and dimmer,
This bitter indifference of the old men,
This exquisite indifference of women.

6

Old men, you will grow stronger and healthier
With broad red cheeks and clear hard eyes—
Are not your meat and drink the choicest?
Blood of the young, dear flesh of the young men?

7

Ah, you women, cruel exquisite women,
What a love-fountain is poured out for you,
What coloured streams for your pleasure!
Go your ways, pass on, forget them;
Give your lips and breasts to the old men,
The kindly, impetuous, glowing, old men!
They who will love you indeed, indeed, dears,
Not as we do, drained of our blood, with weeping,
Sell yourselves, oh, give yourselves to the cripples,
Give yourselves to the weak, the poor forgotten,
Give yourselves to those who escape the torture
And buy their blood from the pools with weight of
    gold.

Give yourselves to them, pass on, forget us;
We, any few that are left, a remnant,
Sit alone together in cold and darkness,
Dare not face the light for fear we discover

The dread woe, the agony in our faces,
Sit alone without sound in bitter dreaming
Of our friends, our dear brothers, the young men,
Who were mangled and abolished, squeezed dry of
blood,
Emptied and cast aside that the lakes might widen,
That the lips of the women might be sweet to the old
men.

8

Go your ways, you women, pass and forget us,
We are sick of blood, of the taste and sight of it;
Go now to those who bleed not and to the old men,
They will give you beautiful love in answer!
But we, we are alone, we are desolate,
Thinning the blood of our brothers with weeping,
Crying for our brothers, the men we fought with,
Crying out, mourning them, alone with our dead
ones;
Praying that our eyes may be blinded
Lest we go mad in a world of scarlet,
Dropping, oozing from the veins of our brothers.

EPILOGUE

Che son contenti nel fuoco

WE are of those that Dante saw
Glad, for love's sake, among the flames of hell,
Outdaring with a kiss all-powerful wrath;
For we have passed athwart a fiercer hell,
Through gloomier, more desperate circles
Than ever Dante dreamed:
And yet love kept us glad.

IMAGES OF DESIRE

PRELUDE

How could I love you more?
I would give up
Even that beauty I have loved too well
That I might love you better.
Alas, how poor the gifts that lovers give—
I can but give you of my flesh and strength,
I can but give you these few passing days
And passionate words that since our speech began
All lovers whisper in all women's ears.

I try to think of some one gift
No lover yet in all the world has found;
I think: If the cold sombre gods
Were hot with love as I am
Could they not endow you with a star
And fix bright youth for ever in your limbs?
Could they not give you all things that I lack?

You should have loved a god; I am but dust.
Yet no god loved as loves this poor frail dust.

AN OLD SONG

I HAVE no lust or care
    To sing of Mary,
I praise the quaint sweet air
    Of a mortal lady.

She is not clothed in sad
    Raiment like Mary,
But in cloth and silk that is glad
    And full seemly.

Her eyes are not tear-rimmed
    Like those of Mary;
Only with love are they dimmed
    When she kisses me.

By God, though she be God's mother,
    I care not for Mary,
Only to serve this other
    That is so dear to me.

EPIGRAMS

1

YOUR mouth is fragrant as an orange-grove
In April, and your lips are hyacinths,
Dark, dew-wet, folded, petalled hyacinths
Which my tongue pierces like an amorous bee.

2

Your body is whiter than the moon-white sea,
More white than foam upon a rocky shore,
Whiter than that white goddess born of foam.

POSSESSION

I MUST possess you utterly
And utterly must you possess me;
So even if that dreamer's tale
Of heaven and hell be true
There shall be two spirits rived together
Either in whatever peace be heaven
Or in the icy whirlwind that is hell
For those who loved each other more than God—
So that the other spirits shall cry out:
'Ah! Look how the ancient love yet holds to them
That these two ghosts are never driven apart
But kiss with shadowy kisses and still take
Joy from the mingling of their misty limbs!'

AN INTERLUDE

THERE is a momentary pause in love
When all the birth-pangs of desire are lulled . . .

I wait,
And glide upon the crested surge of days
Like some sea-god, with tangled, dripping beard
And smooth hard skin, who glimpses from the sea
An earth-girl naked by the long foam fringe,
And, utterly forgetting all his life,
Hurries toward her, glad with sudden love.

Even in that pause of speed I live;
And though the great wave curl in spikes of foam
And crash me bleeding at her cool small feet
All breathless with the water's sudden swirl,
I shall be glad of every stabbing wound
If she will hold my tired limbs to hers
And breathe wild love into my mouth and thrill
Even the blood I shed with that desire
Which throbs all through me at her lightest touch.

ELLA

Ella è quanto di ben può far natura

If I should pass my life
Dead to the beauty of the world,
Not knowing the glint of sunlight,
Wind rustling among deep grasses,
Heavy fall of blossom from spring trees,
Fragrance of southern orange-groves,
Splendour of bronze and lofty spread
Of wide arras in dead kings' dwellings,
Dead to the sound of music
That tears the heart with infinite longing,
Dead to Homer, dead to Dante, dead to Villon,
Dead to all things lovely save her loveliness,
To all beauty but her body's glory,
To all music but her voice speaking,
To all knowledge save of her—
Oh, then, I should have all things amply,
She containing in herself all virtue
Of every fair thing worthy of loving.

HER MOUTH

1

HER mouth is a crushed flower
That unpetals marvellously
Beneath my lips.

2

The perfume of her flesh stays with me
Dwells in my mouth and nostrils
After she has gone,
So that no flavour of wine or flower
Can conquer it.

3

The crimson that dyes her lips
Dyed mine, so close were our kisses;
All day I felt its soft caress
Making smooth my lips.

4

She has but to turn her head
And lay her lips to mine
For all my blood to throb tumultuously:
She is so shudderingly beautiful.

5

When I am bitter sad
With the emptiness of harsh days
The memory of her kissing mouth
Burns me to gladness.

PORTRAIT

1

YOUR body has the hot splendour of gold lands
Laden with sunlight and sharp heat—
Lovely and savage.

2

Hair such as yours
Folded the white brows of Lesbia;
Such subtle weary eyes
Stabbed the young Roman to despair.

3

You are of those whose cruel lips
Cried in the flame-pierced darkness
Curses and prayers to Hecate;
Whose mouths were swift and soft to kiss
And, having kissed, were bitter in revenge.

4

Such little breasts as yours
Felt the quick asp bite
Where lords had pressed their lips.

5

For such as you
Kings have laid down their diadems,
And brave men have shed tears,
And gentle men done secret murder.

6

And you are indifferent to all this,
Weary-eyed and too distraught to care
Whether your hands are wet with tears or blood;
Your eyes strain through a mist of lust
For one face clear with love,
Your lips parch for one kiss of tenderness.

DAYBREAK

THE naked pale limbs of the dawn lie sheathed
    in dove-white folds of lawn
But from one scarlet breast I see the cloudy
    cover slowly drawn.

Not all the blood of all our dead, the bright,
    gay blood so gaily shed,
Shines with so clear a glow as gleams your breast-
    flower from our candid bed.

Ah, bend above me, dear, and take my life breath
    with your lips and break
My body up as wheaten bread, and use my very
    blood to slake

Your parching sudden thirst of lust. Be cruel,
    love, be fierce and thrust
Your white teeth in my flesh and taste how
    honey-sweet is amorous dust.

Ah! slay me with your lips, ah! kill my body's
    strength and spirit's will
So that at dawn I need not go but lie between
    your breast-flowers still.

SLEEP

If but to sleep alone be fair,
  As poets say,
How piercing sweet to lie all night
  Until the day
With all her flower-like body pressed
  Close unto mine,
To feel her moving heart, to taste
  Her breath like wine . . .

Ah, it were good to cease and die
  So sweet a way,
Never to waken from our bed
  To the chill day,
But sleep for ever in a dream,
  Head beside head,
Warm in a golden swoon of love—
  Divinely dead.

RESERVE

Though you desire me I will still feign sleep
And check my eyes from opening to the day,
For as I lie, thrilled by your gold-dark flesh,
I think of how the dead, my dead, once lay.

IMAGES OF DESIRE

1

I DO not even scorn your lovers—
They clasped an image of you, a cloud,
Not the whole life of you that's mine.

2

I do not even pity my mistresses—
Such a poor shadow of desire
Their half-warm passion drew from me.

3

You are a delicate Arab mare
For whom there is but one rider;
I am a sea that takes joyfully
Only one straight ship upon my breast.

4

Like a dark princess whose beauty
Many have sung, you wear me,
The one jewel that is warmed by your breast.

5

As a soldier weary of fighting
Turns for peace to some golden city,
So do I turn to you, beloved.

6

The scarlet that stains your lips and breast-
    points—
Let it be my blood that dyes them,
My very blood so gladly yielded.

7

Let it be your flesh and only your flesh
That fashions for me a child
Whose beauty shall be only less than yours.

8

Everlasting as the sea round the islands
I cry at your door for love;
Everlasting as the unchangeable sea
I cry the infinite for space to love you.

9

Earth of the earth, body of the earth,
Flesh of our mother, life of all things,
A flower, a bird, a rock, a tree,
Thus I love you, sister and lover,
Would that we had one mother indeed
That we might be bound closer by shame.

Love, though the whole earth rock
With the shattering roar of the guns' booming,
Though in that horror of din and flame and murder
All men's blood grows faint and their limbs as water,
Though I return once more to the battle,
Though perhaps I be lost to you for ever—
Give me, O love, your love for this last brief season,
Be mine indeed as I am yours.

Tonight there shall be no tears, no wearing sorrow,
No drawn-out agony of hope, no cold despairing,
Only we two together in a sudden glory
Of infinite delight and sharp sweet yearning,
Shutting out for a space the world's harsh horror.

Kiss my lips with your mouth that is wet with wine,
Wine that is only less keen than your lips are;
Slip from under your fragile garments as a white rose
Slips from under her leaves to the naked sunlight;
Give to my eyes your straight young body,
The limbs that embrace me, the breasts that caress me,
Whisper to me the sudden words of yearning,
The broken words that speak an infinite yearning
That delight would last for ever, love never be ended. . . .

Give me this and I care not if death come after,
For tonight there shall be no tears, no wearing sorrow,
Only our kisses and whispers and stabbing heart-beats.

PRAYER

LORD and father of life,
Of death and of bitter weeping,
One or many, pitiful or cruel,
Hear me, my prayer beating
Like rain importunately, without intermission,
For life, for a little life.

You know not her or love
If you let death take me.

I do not ask you for her—
No god can take her from me,
Take her kisses and lithe body.
Give me life, a few years
To pour out for her,
Until she tires of me
Or age loosens my sinews
And I be no more delightful to her.

Her body is honey and wheat,
The taste of her mouth delicate;
Her eyes overcome me with desire,
Her lips are a woman's.
Under her feet I spread my days
For her walking,
She touches me with her hands
And I am faint with beauty.

Therefore I am not willing to die
Since she needs me.
For her sake I would betray my comrades.
Yet if you are so avid of blood
That even she cannot move you—
Poor god without a lover—
Kill us together, mouth to mouth and happy.

This is not hell—
At least merely a comfortable hell
With warmth and food and some still moments
Ere the true hell comes rushing in again;
Yet this one thought is torture:

Have I lost her, lost her indeed?
Lost the calm eyes and eager lips of love,
The two-fold amorous breasts and braided hair,
The white slim body my senses fed upon
And all the secret shadows shot with fire?

A SOLDIER'S SONG

How sadly for how many nights
My dear will lie alone,
Or lie in other arms than mine
While I lie like a stone.

If she remembers me and weeps
For her lost happiness,
Though dead, I shall be pierced at heart
For her great loneliness.

If she forgets me, if she gives
Her lips and limbs to new desire,
Though dead, I shall be pierced at heart,
Burned stark by a sharp fire.

I would not have her pine and weep,
I would not have her love again—
Whatever comes after I die
There will be only pain and pain.

I dare not ask for life, I dare
Only to ask for utter death
So that I may not know she breathes
Life from another's amorous breath.

ABSENCE

DAY after day fades from me,
Each one cold and wan
Because you are not near me.

Night after night drifts past,
Cheerless, indifferent,
Because you are not with me,
Because I have not your lips to burn me
Awake to a great delight,
Because your eyes are not looking into mine
With the keen entreaty of desire,
Because each night I lie alone.

I am fierce, indignant, humiliated—
To be chained away from you
When I desire you above all things.
Half I possess you, half hold you, half keep you—
But would all of you satisfy my desire?

I am insatiate, desperate—
Death, if need be, or you near me,
Loving me, beautifully piercing me to life,
But not this, not this bitterness, this grief,
This long desert of absence.

GAIN

LET not the jesting bitter gods
Who sit so goldenly aloof from us
Mock us too deeply,
Let them not boast they hold alone
The reins of pleasure, the delight of lust—
We also, we that are but air and dust,
Moistening that dust a little with old wine
And kindling that air with fire of love,
Have burned an hour or two with blossoming
    pangs,
And, leaning on soft breasts made keen with
    love
And murmuring fierce words of rending bliss,
Have gathered turn by turn unto our lips
The twin wild roses of delight,
The quick flower-flames that sear into the soul
Sharp wounds of pleasure and extreme desire.

CYNTHIA

Day droops on stems of pallid light
Over these sodden northern fields,
    And I am lonely, thinking here,
        Cynthia, of you.

Here life is but a phantom of himself
And limps and mutters by these war-worn paths,
    And I could weep to waste my youth,
        Cynthia, from you.

O rose that filled my mouth with life!
Wine of your lips, your budded breasts!
    How could I serve another god,
        Cynthia, but you?

THE WINTER PARK

I⊤ is dreary
Out in the park of the *chateau;*
The paths are deep in mud,
The trees damp and *tristes;*
The marble stairs by the lake-side
Are stained with mould,
Untidy with twigs and dead grass;
There are no swans left
To stud the blue water
With their languid silver;
Oh, it is desolate and mournful and lifeless
Under the soundless trees
By the waveless water,
But a frame for my gay dreams
Of your head bent back
With lips unfolded for my mouth to kiss!

MEDITATION

Outside the young frost crisps the grass
And bends the narrow willow boughs
And flecks the dyke with little spears of ice;
The huge moon, yellow and blotched,
Like the face of a six days' corpse,
Stares hideously over the barren wood.

In the silence, the deep pool-like silence,
Untroubled by crash of guns or tramp of men,
I sit alone in a small Belgian house
And stare against the moon and feel
Silence like a slow wave of the outer sea
Drive over and through me,
Purging out bitterness, effacing miseries.

I have what I yearned for—
The chance to live my life out to the end.
And it is a great joy to sit here quietly and think
That soon I shall return to her and say:
'Now it is a free man that kisses you'.
There will be strange meetings in cities for me,
The hush of summer in English gardens,
The glitter of spring in Italy,
The old cafés in Paris.

And I shall have books again,
Long quiet evenings by the tranquil lamp,
Or wild gaiety with 'my own sort'—
And always there will be her love,
Her eyes holding me dumb,
Her mouth drawing the blood to my lips.

And yet and yet
I am still not free from bitterness,
For as I sit here thinking so tenderly of her,
Maybe, over there across the Channel,
Her eyes smile at another man
As they smiled at me,
And her red mouth stabs him to passion
As it stabbed me.
Is any woman both beautiful and loyal?

I think also that I am too restless
For the old life,
Too contemptuous of narrow shoulders
To sit again with the café-chatterers,
Too sick at heart with overmuch slaughter
To dream quietly over books,
Too impatient of lies to cajole
Even my scanty pittance from the money-vultures.

Perhaps, then, this is my happiest moment,
Here in this cold little Belgian house,
Remembering harsh years past,
Plotting gold years to come,
Trusting so blithely in a woman's faith;
In the quiet night,
In the silence.

ODELETTE

Now I regret
The fervour that has gone from me,
Stolen by circumstance,
Leaving me lassitude—
A deserted temple with no god.

Could I not blind you
With sudden enchantment,
Making life a phantasm of delight?

Sharp clusters of flowers—
Light irradiates the city;
O distant perfume
Of lands intangible
That vanish ere we reach them!
O sudden shouting
Of the great rowers, straining
Bronze backs through the wave-track!
Clamour about us,
The interminable traffic
Of a mistress city!

I come from darkness
And ways of dolour
To the brilliance of my city;
I am glad of her ways,
Her harshness, her beauty,
Her wise old brooding,
Her mysterious person.

And you are unhappy,
And I cannot gladden you—

Misery of lovers.

EPILOGUE

HAVE I spoken too much or not enough of love?
Who can tell?

But we who do not drug ourselves with lies
Know, with how deep a pathos, that we have
Only the warmth and beauty of this life
Before the blankness of the unending gloom.
Here for a little while we see the sun
And smell the grape-vines on the terraced hills,
And sing and weep, fight, starve and feast, and
    love
Lips and soft breasts too sweet for innocence.
And in this little glow of mortal life—
Faint as one candle in a large cold room—
We know the clearest light is shed by love,
That when we kiss with life-blood in our lips,
Then we are nearest to the dreamed-of gods.

EXILE

EXILE

Do you dwell on the snowy promontory of Mimas?

How shall we utter
This horror, this rage, this despair?
How shall we strike at baseness,
Cut through disgust with scorn?
How rend with slashed fingers
The bars and walls of the lives
Which blacken the air and pure light?

What are they? Alien, brutish,
Base seed of Earth's ravished womb.
Shall we yield our light and our truth—
The flash of the helm,
And the foam-grey eyes and the hair
Braided with gold,
Steel mail on a firm breast?
Shall we yield?

Their life, their truth?
O laugh of disdain!
If ours be a goddess
Chaste, proud, and remote,
What is theirs?
A boastful woman, a whore,
One greasy of flesh, stale
With hot musty perfume—
While ours—
Firm-fleshed as the treeless hills,
With her rigid breasts and hard thighs,
Cold and perfect and fresh—
Fields crisp with new frost—
Sets the violet-crown in her hair,
Turns an unstained brow to the sky.

Let us stand by the earth-shaking sea
Unfurrowed by a hull,
Let us move among beeches and oaks
Unprofaned by loud speech;
Let us reverence the sacred earth
And the roar of unbridled falls
And the crash of an untamed sea.
Let us shade our eyes from the sun
And gaze through the leaves,
Far, most far—
Shall we see her hill
And the marble front of her house
And herself, standing calm,
Many-coloured, triumphant, austere?

EUMENIDES

It is at night one thinks,
At night, staring with sleepless eyes
At the narrow moonlit room.
Outside the owls hoot briefly,
And there are stars
Whose immortal order makes one shudder.

I do not need the ticking of my watch
To tell me I am mortal;
I have lived with, fed upon death
As happier generations feed on life;
My very mind seems gangrened.

What am I, lying here so still,
Staring till I almost see the silence?
What am I?
What obscure fragment of will?
What paltry life cell?

Have I not striven and striven for health?
Lived calmly (as it seemed) these many months,
Walked daily among neat hedged fields,
Watched the long pageant of the clouds,
Loved, drawn into my being, flowers,
English flowers—the thin anemones,
The honey drops of tufted primroses,
Wild scented hyacinths, white stitchwort,
The spotted orchis, tall scentless violets,
Larch buds, green and scarlet,
Noted the springing green
Of white ash, birch and heavy oak,
Lived with the noblest books, the noblest friends,
Looked gay, laughed free, worked long?

I have done all this,
And yet there are always nights
I lie awake staring with sleepless eyes,
And what is my mind's sickness,
What the agony I struggle with,
I can hardly tell.

Loos, that horrible night in Hart's Crater,
The damp cellars of Maroc,
The frozen ghostly streets of Vermelles,
That first night-long gas bombardment—
O the thousand images I see
And struggle with and cannot kill—
That boot I kicked
(It had a mouldy foot in it)
The night K's head was smashed
Like a rotten pear by a mortar,
The other night I trod on the dead man
And all the officers were hit . . .

These, like Eumenides, glide about me,
Fearful memories of despair and misery,
Tortured flesh, caked blood, endurance,
Men, men and the roar of shells,
The hissing lights, red, green, yellow,
The clammy mud, the tortuous wire,
The slippery boards . . .

It is all so stale,
It has been said a thousand times;
Millions have seen it, been it, as I;
Millions may be haunted by these spirits
As I am haunted;
May feel, as I feel, in the darkness,
Their flesh dripping into corruption,

Their youth and love and gaiety
Dissolved, violently slain, annihilated.

What is it I agonise for?
The dead? They are quiet;
They can have no complaint.
No, it is my own murdered self—
A self which had its passion for beauty,
Some moment's touch with immortality—
Violently slain, which rises up like a ghost
To torment my nights,
To pain me.
It is myself that is the Eumenides,
That will not be appeased, about my bed;
It is the wrong that has been done me
Which none has atoned for, none repented of,
Which rises before me, demanding atonement.

Tell me, what answer shall I give my murdered self?

LE MAUDIT

WOMEN'S tears are but water;
The tears of men are blood.

He sits alone in the firelight
And on either side drifts by
Sleep, like a torrent whirling,
Profound, wrinkled, and dumb.

Circuitously, stealthily,
Dawn occupies the city;
As if the seasons knew of his grief,
Spring has suddenly changed into snow.

Disaster and sorrow
Have made him their pet;
He cannot escape their accursed embraces.
For all his dodgings
Memory will lacerate him.

What good does it do to wander
Night hours through city streets?
Only that in poor places
He can be with common men
And receive their unspoken
Instinctive sympathy.
What has life done for him?
He stands alone in the darkness
Like a sentry never relieved,
Looking over a barren space,
Awaiting the tardy finish.

BONES

Now when this coloured curious web
Which hides my awkward bones from sight
Unrolls, and when the thing that's I—
A pinch of lighted dust that flashes—
Has somehow suddenly gone out,
What quaint adventures may there be
For my unneeded skeleton?

Some men's bones are left (like trees
Which cannot move from where they root)
On open hills or low damp hollows,
Wherever war has struck them down;
And some bones after many years
A waggish bomb digs up, and strews—
Thigh bones and ribs mixed up with coffins—
About a well-bombarded town;
And some are plunged with ancient wreckage
Where fishes with blue bulging eyes

Slide past, and clouds of tiniest shells
In ages make a rocky cover;
And some lie here and some lie there
Until they moulder quite away;
Some in the village garth and some
In quiet suburban labelled rows;
And some are powdered up in fire
And some are shown in dull museums. . . .

Now, while his flesh remains, a man
Is something; but who feels akin
To any nameless poor old bones?
Even she, who with miraculous lips
Set little flowering plots of kisses

Over our body, will not care
To hug us when our bones are dry;
And she who carried us nine months
And built them with her vital blood
Might pass them by and never know
These were the bones so hard to bear;
And likelier still, our dearest child
Would scorn to know us so unveiled,
Unwilling to believe his flesh,
Still firm and petal-sweet, was bred
By such a pitiful old wreck.

But, in the end, the bones go too,
And drift about as dust which hangs
In a long sun-shaft, or dissolve
Into the air to help build up
The pulpy tissues of fine leaves
Or heavier flakes of ruddy flesh,
Or even someone else's bones.

I leave to those superior minds
Who make theology their care
The task of settling whose shall be
These much-used frameworks at the last;
I rather see a wearier world
Shed, æons hence, its comely flesh
To dance, a mournful skeleton,
Sedately round a dingier sun.

MEDITATION

As I sit here alone in the calm lamplight,
Watching the red embers
Slowly fade and crumble into grey dust,
With that impenetrable silence
Of long night about me
And the companionship of the immemorial dead
At hand upon my shelves,
Then, when I have freed myself
From trivial designs and false longings,
When I have fortified my soul
To endure the rough shock of truth,
Then I can think without trembling or whimpering
That I must see you dead,
That I must press down your useless eyelids,
Extend your arms, smooth down your hair,
And set upon your lips a withered flower,
The poor last kiss.

In the imagination
I have endured all that without a tear;
Yet, if it were not that above all things
I seek and cling to my own truth,
I would cozen my agony with any lie,
Any far-fetched similitude, any dream
Which would lighten with hope this heavy
    certitude;
I would kiss the feet of man or woman
Who would prove to me your immortality,
Prove to me your new life circles this life
As the immense sky, naked and starry,
Circles with its illimitable round
The low white roof of our cottage.

Yet, as I would not catch your love with a lie,
But force you to love me as I am,
Faulty, imperfect, human,
So I would not cheat your inward being
With untrue hopes nor confuse pure truth with
  a legend.
This only I have:
I am true to my truth, I have not faltered;
And my own end, the sudden departure
From the virile earth I love so eagerly,
Once such a sombre matter, now appears nothing
Beside this weightier, more torturing bereavement.

IN THE PALACE GARDEN

THE yews became a part of me,
The long walks edged with sparse flowers,
The fluttering green fringes of elm trees
Blurring the washed blue sky,
The long shivering ripples of the river,
Bird-calls, all we saw and did,
Became me, built me up,
Helped me to love you.
I was happy.
It was enough not to be dead,
Not to be a black spongy mass of decay
Half-buried on the edge of a trench,
More than enough to be young and gay,
To know my lips were such
Yours would be glad to meet them.
I loved you with my old miseries
Which were no longer miseries,
With the scent of the lilacs
And the softly sprinkling fountain,
And the kind glances of passers.
How did it happen then?
The sun did not cease shining,
The water rippled just as fleetly,
I loved you just as indiscreetly—
But gradually my golden mood tarnished,
Happiness hissed into nothing—
Metal under a fierce acid—
And I was whispering:
'This happiness is not yours;
It is stolen from other men.
Coward! You have shirked your fate'.

EPITAPH IN BALLADE FORM

Which Villon made for Himself and his Friends Waiting to be hanged with Them

BROTHERS among men who after us shall live,
Let not your hearts' disdain against us rise,
For if some pity for our woe ye have,
The sooner God your pardon shall devise.
Behold, here five or six of us we peise;
As to our flesh, which we fed wantonly,
Rotten, devoured, it hangeth mournfully;
And we, the bones, to dust and ash are riven,
Let none make scorn of our infirmity,
But pray to God that all we be forgiven.

If, brothers, we cry out, ye should not give
Disdain for answer, even if justice 'tis
That murders us. This thing ye should believe,
That always all men are not wholly wise;
Pray often for us then, not once or twice,
Before the fair son of the Virgin Mary,
Lest that—for us—his grace prove injury
And we beneath the lord of hell be driven.
Now we are dead, cease importunity
And pray to God that all we be forgiven.

The rain doth weaken all our strength and lave
Us, the sun blackens us again and dries;
Our eyes the ravens hollow like a grave;
Our beards and eyebrows are plucked off by pies.
Never rest comes to us in any wise;
Now here, now there, as the wind sways, sway we;

Swung at the wind's high pleasure ceaselessly,
More pecked by birds than hazel nuts that ripen.
Be ye not then of our fraternity,
But pray to God that all we be forgiven.

Envoi

Prince Jesus, above all hast mastery,
Let not high hell become our seignory;
There we have nought to do nor order even.
Brothers, keep here no thought of mockery,
But pray to God that all we be forgiven.

STAND here a moment, friend,
And look across the silent garnered fields;
See how they turn like huge-limbed country
    gods,
Their labour ended, to a solemn rest—
A rest so like to death that if they think
Their thoughts are those that are befitting death.
With them is peace,
Peace of bland misty skies and hushed winds
Steadily whispering comfort above them,
Peace of the slowly-rising tranquil moon,
Peace of the sombre woods whose leaves,
Heavily drooping, pine but fall not yet;
Peace that the fruit is plucked, the wheatstalks
    shorn,
And entered all the increase of the year,
Peace, humble but august.

Would you not joy to share in such a mood,
The long task fitly ended, peace at heart,
Under such skies, at such an hour as this?

O friend, why is it that the fields have peace
And we have none? I press my hands
Softly against my aching eyes and feel
How hot they are with scanning many books;
My brain is dry with thoughts of many men,
My heart is faint with deaths of many gods.
I know I live only because I suffer.
I know of truth only because I seek,
Only because I need it know I love.

Hunters of truth and wisdom!
O friend, who sped that bitter speech?
What soft-tongued foe whispered that dear
    deceit?
We have hunted, you and I, these many years;
Either the game is scant, the luck is thwart,
Or we are mole-eyed or the gods are cruel,
For what we seized breathless with joy
Turned rotten in our hands and what we missed
Seemed ever the one quarry that we sought.

No need to answer. I know, I know
All you would say; I know our search
Is nobler than the common tumult;
We are nearer the gods than those who run and
    fly.
The shadows we pursue may not be shadows,
The dreams we live with may be more than
    dreams . . .
All this I hope; but when the autumn comes
And heavy carts sway loaded to the barns,
And swallows gather to be gone, and rooks
Flock to the fields for scattered grain,
O friend, I am filled with musing and distrust,
So poor my harvest to this golden wealth,
So teased my spirit to this opulent peace.

Come, what were you saying of Lucretius?

DEADNESS of English winter, dreariness,
cold sky over provincial towns, mist.
Melancholy of undulating trams
solitary jangling through muddy streets,
narrowness, imperfection, dullness,
black extinguisher over English towns;
mediocre women in dull clothes—
their nudity a disaster—
heavy cunning men (guts and passbooks),
relics of gentry, workmen on bicycles,
puffy small whores, baby carriages,
shops, newspapers, bets, cinemas, allotments . . .

These are your blood; their begetters
made in the same bed as yours
(horror of copulation),
colossal promiscuity of flesh through centuries
(seed and cemeteries).
Sculptor! show Mars
bloody in gas-lit abattoirs,
Apollo organist of Saint Mary's,
Venus of High Street, Athena,
worshipped at National schools.
Painter! there are beets in allotments,
embankments, coal-yards, villas, grease,
interpret the music, orchestra,
trams, trains, cars, hobnails, factories—
O poet! chant them to the pianola,
to the metronome in faultless verse . . .

FREEDOM

At last, after many years, I am saturated
With pity and agony and tears;
At last I have reached indifference;
Now I am almost free—
A gold pellet of sunlight
Dropped, curdling, into green water.

The grass, which is one with our flesh
And bends like an old man
Back to the mould, their mother,
Beckons with long fingers
The poplar nymphs and white ash dryads
To caress their white feet dancing,
Weightless, pale, and immortal.

The dead may be myriad,
But my nostrils are sweet with crushed leaves,
My eyes clear as flowers,
My hands stainless;
About me is opulent light
That drenches the lightless sea,
Piercing shadowy windless places
Where sea-moss fringes quiet pebbles.

Over harsh slopes the centaurs gallop
With whistling manes, a rattle of hoofs;
White shapes rustle the dew-dripping thickets,
Slim fauns dance by the grass track.
I have passed through hate and pity,
Desire and anguish to this:
I am myself,
I am free.

RETREAT

LET there be silence sometimes,
A space of starless night—
A silence, a space of forgetfulness
Away from seething of lives,
The rage of struggle.

Let there be a time of retreat,
A hiding of the sun and all colours,
For the soul to ride at ease in darkness;
For the coldness of no-life
To soothe life's burning.

Let there be rest
For wearied eyes to ease their labour
And wander across great distances,
For the spirit to slip the chain of hours
And drift in Atlantic waves of time.

Grant peace;
For a space let there be no roar
Of wheels and voices, no din
Of steel and stone and fire.
Let us cleanse ourselves from the sweat and dirt,
Let us be hushed, let us breathe
The cold sterile wind from colourless space.

HAVING SEEN MEN KILLED

When by chance
As I turn up the brow of the hill,
At a glance
I perceive there's a new grave to fill,
And I see all the poor apparatus of death—

The straight hole
And the planks and the lowering rope;
And the toll
Of the bell and the mirage of hope
In the words
Duly mumbled for those that remain—

Then I smile
'Fine morning', nod to the sexton's nod,
For a while
Wonder if Einstein proves or disproves God,
But how soon
Find myself cheerfully humming a tune.

NIGHTINGALE

Night winds beat my naked flesh,
Waves of air rush over me.
The young moon stands among frozen clouds;
Far off as death burn the ice-sparkles which are
   stars
A wall of rough black pine
Cuts the pale sky.

Your voice—
Ah, chastest, coldest thing!
The brief shrill clang of ice on glass,
The note of fragile metal sharply struck,
The lapse of waters.
Ah, virginal delight!
The woods hold you
And the boughs frozen with dew.

This is no love-song,
No breath of wind and summer flowers,
No murmur of desire;
But such a hymn,
Fierce, lonely and untamed,
As the Trœzenian hunter sang
Before the marble shrine.

So wild a song once rose
From the women of Artemis
In some cold hidden valley
Where trees sombrely ringed
A black lake and cold mist glided
As the first moonrays
Glittered through clouds.

Those foam-frail girls
Greek sailors saw beyond their prows,
Whose flesh was cooled by the waves' heart,
Whose veins ran spray of the storm,
Sang this song
As dawn stood grey on the sea's rim.

But this is no love-song,
No echo of kisses.

PAPILLONS

(*Ballet Russe*)

WHAT phantasm of the heart of men
So whitely and so wanly
Gibes at us?

Fool!
Had your heart the warmth
That burns in the thin candle-heart,
You had not lost her.

White—
As one who trembles at her golden scorn—
You ask for treachery.

Be red, be blood-red, brother,
And she'll not dare
To dance to other colder lips than yours!

TRUTH

TRUTH! if my words grow wan and cold
The fault is yours.
Yet what a fool was I,
Like the farm zany in the nursery tale,
To barter a full bag of coined fancies
For your lean scrip of verities.
What a mouldy cheat was this!
Truth, I suspect your dwelling-place
Is round about old graves and wormy tombs
Inscribed *Cras tibi, hodie mihi;*
I never met you at a kindly feast
Or with a friend before a blazing fire
Or walking in the sunshine as I sang.
But books, books—cursed croaking sirens—
Written by old men moping at their aches,
Or young men skilled in acids and despair,
Vaunted you, described you,
Offered to impart you for a fee.

There are fools and fools:
Gay fools whose hours pass merrily
And solemn, nasty fools
Whose dismal witchcraft
Makes pigsties of our marriage-beds,
    Schedules the spring,
    Cuts flowers in zinc,
    Turns wine to ink,
    Lops poor Puck's wing.

O Satan! You've disguised yourself as Truth
And made a solemn fool of more than me;
But by these presents, firmly weighed and penned,
I here renounce you and your verminous tricks.

Come, happy Falsehood,
Once again,
Make me a merry fool.

THE PARROT

I SHALL buy a parrot,
I shall call it Maude Cambronne;
It shall be present at all my Waterloos.
Snap loud, parrot.

We shall drift upon the river
And read romantic books
To the music of a record
Playing César Franck or Strauss;
Snap loud, parrot.

Cynical, explosive parrot,
Are you honest as you're shrill?
Do you lure me, feathered Faustus,
Down the tarry paths of hell?
Snap loud, parrot.

Do I live for copulation?
Do I live for ham and wine?
O my parrot, raven-hearted,
O my parrot, not yet mine?
Snap loud, parrot.

When I air my witless folly,
When I dogmatise in print,

When I lull the shuddering terrors
With a cradle-tune of cant;
Snap loud, parrot.

Parrot, when I'm half-successful,
When I think I'm rather good,
When I'm half inclined to purchase
Half-indulgences from God,
Snap loud, parrot.

I shall buy a parrot,
I shall call it Maude Cambronne;
It shall be present at all my Waterloos.
Snap loud, parrot.

TO THOSE WHO PLAYED FOR SAFETY
IN LIFE

I ALSO might have worn starched cuffs,
Have gulped my morning meal in haste,
Have clothed myself in dismal stuffs
Which prove a sober City taste;

I also might have rocked and craned
In undergrounds for daily news,
And watched my soul grow slowly stained
To middle-class unsightly hues . . .

I might have earned ten pounds a week!

WORDS FOR MUSIC

1

Suffer my too ambitious hand
    To range these low delicious hills,
Invest me freedman of a land
    Exile from which dejects and kills;
With pious lips let me revere
The sacred roses cherished here.

I'll gather no more garlands now—
    Mere bubbles of imperfect light—
Since in that secret country grow
    Petals so delicate and light.
And when for love of flowers I pine,
My senses shall exult o'er thine.

2

Unlike that ancient Teian boaster
    And those who ape his senile lies,
I cannot show a monstrous roster
    Of ladies captive to my eyes.

Yet five or six I might discover
    (Did grateful prudence not restrain)
Who felt a pleasure-giving lover
    Should not be cut, but come again.

If this were ill, may they forgive me;
    They never seemed to take alarm;
Whate'er John Wesley says, believe me,
    Women know best what does them harm.

3

Euphemia studies law, Aminta
    Inspects the ailments of the poor,

Eudocia prays and Araminta
   Numbers the stars on heaven's floor;
Yet Chloe for my mistress I decree,
Whose only art is artless love of me.

'Tis not the statute binds together,
   Physic ignores the wounds we share,
Love works in dull or starry weather
   And nakedness suits not with prayer;
Then let your learning, Chloe, still consist
In all the various ways of being kist.

4

Believe not, Chloe, all your grace
Can dwell within that lovely face,
Believe not all your beauty lies
In the mild prison of those eyes.

Yet, Chloe, think not I incline
To passions abstract and divine,
'Tis not a soul alone could move
This ardent flesh to sue for love.

But when that rose-tipped breast I see,
Or the white splendour of your knee,
I covet a more precious fleece
Than ever Jason brought to Greece.

5

When to Dorinda I impart
      My passion,
She vows the mistress of my heart
      Is fashion,
That Celia, Chloe, and Lucinda
Shall never rule with proud Dorinda.

I crave more beauties than do stir

My vision;
For all reply she shows me her
Derision.
Must I then suffer this, a martyr,
That dares not rise above her garter?

If she persists a prude, I swear
I'll leave her
Till some chaste, clumsy cuckold dare
Relieve her;
As heavy guns take virgin trenches,
So husbands smooth our way to wenches.

6

Pulvis et umbra! Chloe, why
Quench my desire with ill-bred gloom,
Since many an amorous death we die
Ere we are born to lie
Loveless and chilly in th' uncomely tomb?
Why, pretty fool, is that a tear
Wronging the cheek I kissed so late?
There is no dust nor shadow here;
Come, kiss me without fear,
And let me bring you to the ivory gate.

7

Daphnis, pray breathe this pastoral vein;
Strew not my broidered sheets with flowers
Dripping cold rain;
Can any civil maid embrace
Daffodils dropped in freezing showers
That soil her lace?
Be (if you choose) a poet but
Expect to find my window shut;
Though Chloe loves whene'er she can,
She loves no pseudo-shepherd-man.

8

Chloe, the gods are too remote
   From this unruly cloud-wrapped ball,
Too tranquil, as the rose-leaves float
   On wine-cups in th' Olympian hall,
To keep a watch on you and me
And frown at lost virginity.

The rose must shed its fragile flower
   Before the slim red fruit appears,
Unloose your garments like a shower
   Of falling petals, quit your fears,
And suffer my religious hand
To pluck the fruit no eye has scanned.

9

O reverend sir, cease to upbraid
   A simple man who lives by reason,
Who never tried to thwart your trade
   By dull invectives out of season:

Desist, then, from your dreary labour;
   I know the errors of my life;
But, though I do not love my neighbour,
   How often have I loved his wife!

10

Sir Pious, pray you hide your eyes;
   By all the saints! you shall not look;
For yonder where the sunshine lies
   Chloe is bathing in the brook:

Chloe is bathing in the brook
   And glads a pagan sight like mine;
But you, Sir Pious, con your book
   And learn that pearls are not for swine.

SONGS FOR SENSUALISTS

A SOPHISTRY OF DURATION

TELL me not beauty dies like dew
  The envious sun draws trembling up,
Nor liken hers to that brief hue
  Flushes the rose's tender cup—
For things like her so lovely are
They should outlive the bravest star.

If all my senses still conspire,
  Ere their meridian be past,
To set the blossoms of desire,
  The worm shall not exult at last;
Her children and my words I trust
Shall speak her grace when we are dust.

A GARDEN HOMILY

Come, thrust your hands in the warm earth
  And feel her strength through all your veins,
Breathe her full odours, taste her mirth
  That laughs away imagined pains.
Touch here life's very womb, but know
This substance makes your grave also.

Shrink not; your flesh is no more sweet
  Than flowers which daily blow and die;
Nor are your mien and dress so neat;
  Nor half so pure your lucid eye.
And yet—by flowers and earth I swear
You're neat and pure, and sweet and fair.

Go tell the shepherd's star, when first
  The evening fans her spark awake,
That light is murderous and accurst—
  But say not Delia faith can break.

Tell the wild rose, when tranquil days
  Have charmed a thousand petals wide,
Tomorrow scatters all her praise—
  But say not Delia's kisses lied.

Swear anything that's monstrous, swear
  That truth is a fantastic lie,
Take oath that Delia is not fair—
  But, oh! that she is false, deny.

MADRIGAL

Oh, by what rite shall I upbraid
  Beauty that will not let me rest?
What charm shall make to fade
  Those cheeks as fragrantly demure as morn
And quench the perfume of her flowering breast?
  All night I waked forlorn,
          I waked forlorn,
Hearkening the lamentation of the rain,
But daylight brought no slumber to my pain,
          no slumber to my pain.

METRICAL EXERCISES

THE BERKSHIRE KENNET

Amongst his hills and holts, as on his way he makes,
At Reading once arrived, clear Kennet overtakes
His lord, the stately Thames. . . .
                                 [Drayton's Polyolbion]

TURN from the city's poisoned air
And dwell with me a little where
The Kennet, gently flowing, speeds
His scent of green and bruised reeds
And water-mints that root in mud,
Cordial and faint; or where his flood
Breaks in a low perpetual roar
Beneath the weir, abrupt and hoar
With ragged foam and trembling spray
Whose perfume damps the hottest day
With cool invisible sweet breath.

Old willows, stout, but near their death,
In winter wave their naked boughs
Beside the stream that roughly ploughs
The loose earth from their roots; in spring
Winds lighter than the swallow's wing
Touch their pale fluttering leaves which throw
A green light on the stream below.
The water-meadows, cool and lush,
Fringed with the ragged hawthorn bush,
Bear lonely elms with shaggy stems—
Green petticoats with ruffled hems—
And oaks in distant clumps, as round
As Latin domes, and poplars sound
And tall as Lombard bell-towers, and

Long aspen screens on either hand.
And all the river's way is lined
With broad reeds rustling in the wind,
And flowers that bend as if they gave
Farewells to every passing wave—
Tall meadow-sweet spreads out as stiff
As Queen Anne's pocket-handkerchief;
And amid willow-herb the sprays
Of loosestrife gold or purple blaze;
And August sees the guelder-rose
Hung with her clustered fruit that glows
Robust and crimson, where in June
Gleamed whiter than the ashen moon
The cold and delicate flowers that shine
Upon the thorny eglantine.
And far across the fields and marsh
The peewit clamours shrill and harsh,
Or—out of sight he wings so high—
The snipe falls drumming from the sky,
Or wary redshanks flit and flute
Clear notes to hush their young brood mute.

O solitude, O innocent peace,
Silence, more precious than the Fleece
That Jason and his fellows sought,
Our greatest riches though unbought,
And hard to find and ill to praise
In noisy and mechanic days!
Yet in these humble meadows they
Have cleansed the wounds of war away,
And brought to my long troubled mind
The health that I despaired to find,
And, while their touch erased the pain,
Breathed the old raptures back again
And in their kindness gave to me

Almost that vanished purity.
Here where the osiers barely sigh
Hour upon hour still let me lie,
Where neither cannon roar nor noise
Of heavy wheels my ears annoys,
And there is none my face to scan
Save some incurious countryman;
And in my cool and hushèd nook
I read some old and gentle book
Until in thought I lift my eyes
To rest on dappled English skies,
And hear the stream go murmuring by
And watch the bubbling eddies fly
As Kennet's waters glide for ever
To wed the elder, nobler river . . .
As on the verge of sleep I nod
I see the ancient river god
Lean on his smooth and polished urn;
His hair is twined with rush and fern
And in his beard are waving reeds
And in his hand are lily seeds.
Ever the marble urn expels
Cool water, pure as that which wells
From some untainted northern hill;
Ever his languid hands do spill
The flowers that nod and dip and smile
Along his banks mile upon mile,
Nor ever do his green eyes shun
The glances of his grateful son.

And if I now invoke him here,
What supercilious lip dare sneer,
What heart that never loved the earth
Dare turn my piety to mirth,
And what vile truckler to the crowd

Scorn me, who live remote and proud?
Then, noble river, take my praise
And grant me more such happy days,
Each evening bring untroubled sleep
As your own waters still and deep,
And let my wealth be more or less,
So it suffice for happiness,
And keep in my untroubled life
The kindness of a comely wife,
And let the years I have been lent
Bring me not fame but sweet content,
And when my days run out and I
Must go, then teach me how to die,
To leave my well-loved solitude
For an enduring quietude.

A WINTER NIGHT

Now the calm acres where I lay
Through half a murmurous summer's day,
Nodding in these drowsy meads
To the curtseying of the reeds,
Are drenched and mournful, harsh and wild.
Hostile to his late spoil'd child,
The turbid river seems to sulk
And hoarsely pours his swollen bulk;
Blind with swirling leaves, the year
Dreads the mort-sheet drawing near,
Cowering hides his frosted head
And mourns his April splendours fled.
The pattering rain falls loud and thick,

Quelling the old clock's gentle tick;
The tossing willows hiss and creak
As if long anguish forced them speak
And curse the loud tormenting gale;
And as their branches groan and wail,
The ivy taps the latticed pane;
The wind howls; and it taps again.

'Clap-to the doors, tomorrow pray';
Tonight be given to mirth and play;
Shut out the wind, shut out the cold,
Shut out the world that's mean and old,
Shut out its madness, but admit
Beauty and memory and wit.

What glowing spirits deign to dwell
Here in this narrow, low-pitched cell,
What stately pleasures I command
With all Eliza's wits at hand!
And how it charms my amorous looks
To see such ranks of noble books—
For some sweet god to ease man's curse
Gave him the gift of choice old verse;
And those whom dull rich men despise
Taste real revenge by growing wise:
Thus even in hell they ease their pain
With Shakespeare, Marlowe and Montaigne.
Then let me sit and entertain
The fancies that invest my brain,
That wheel and flutter hour by hour
Like moths about a campion flower
On heavy dewless nights of May;
And let them poise and wheel and play,
Fan their pattern'd wings, then soar
To the haunts they kept before,

Leaving in my mind and heart
Coloured dust as they depart . . .

And if I tell these fancies? Then
I should be scorn'd by stupid men;
Too well I know both friends and foes
Ever to let my heart unclose,
Ever to give what I should keep
A secret to myself and Sleep.
What! give again, as I have given,
Things sacred sent to me from heaven?
No! though my outward life be rude
It keeps the grace of solitude;
No wealthy fool, no titled whore
Passes this quiet cottage door,
No noisy flatterer of the mob
Warms by my Spartan chimney hob!
But O you distant gods that dwell
Somewhere in earth or heaven or hell,
Turn for a moment from his betters
To hear a proud poor man of letters;
Grant that by toil which flatters none
I earn my needs, and that toil done,
Grant me to live still undisturbed;
Keep this proud spirit yet uncurbed;
Leave me my books and peace and health
And heavier wits may plod for wealth;
Let me ne'er lose an honest friend
And keep me free until the end.

A FOOL I' THE FOREST

A PHANTASMAGORIA

A fool! a fool! I met a fool i' the forest

NOTE

THE application of this phantasmagoria will be apparent when the symbolical nature of the three characters—'I', Mezzetin, the Conjuror—is explained.

The trio are one person split into three.

'I' is intended to be typical of a man of our own time, one who is by temperament more fitted for an art than a scientific civilisation. He is shown at a moment of crisis, and the phantasmagoria is the mirror of his mind's turmoil as he struggles to attain a harmony between himself and the exterior world.

Mezzetin comes from the *Commedia dell' Arte*. He symbolises here the imaginative faculties—art, youth, satire, irresponsible gaiety, liberty. He is one or several of these by turns and all together.

In a similar manner the Conjuror symbolises the intellectual faculties—age, science, righteous cant, solemnity, authority— which is why I make him so malicious.

R. A.

CONTENTS

1

'COURT-JESTER to an age that lacks a King.'
Now who said that?
Some fool who thought the crowd should praise his verses
Instead of punting mildly at the races?
No matter. I'll have a jester—
Like a guilty King who hates his thoughts—
To sing, to play the zany,
Show me the world's an idiot jest,
Cloud-Cuckoo-Land without a Socrates.
When I sit alone
Thoughts of ten thousand perished gods
Tease like a letter I forgot to write;
The good man's wisdom
Mads like a buzzing bee against the pane.
Send me a jester, send me Mezzetin,
Brighella, Feste, Bagatino, Trivelin;
No matter whom, but let him be a fool.

'Las! Good sir, Don Cocodrillo sits in Parliament;
Zirzabella's a Malthusian; Arlequin,
Pale, hungry Arlequin's a bank director,
So ragged and so starved 'twould break your heart, sir;
Pantalone is a reverend judge;
The rest are convicts.
Jupiter was jailed last year for bigamy
And Helen's married to a Guggenheim.
(Sweet Helen, make me immortal with a kiss.)
All lost, all gone, sir, except me,
Poor patient Scaramuccia,
At your service, sir.'

Scaramouch, I hate you.
You're too fat and clean to be a fool.

Where are your lantern jaw and lousy hair,
Your squint, your grin, your burst-out shoes,
Your miserably squeaking voice that uttered oracles?
I want a fool,
A true, a bitter fool, who's looked at life
And sees it's naught, who knows the rich man's *tare*
That eats into his bosom like a cancer,
Knows where the shoe pinches the lovely dame—
But you're no fool, you're washed and fed;
Confess now, on the honour of a charlatan,
You've lectured in America?
I thought as much. Take him away.
I want a fool, a fool, a fool.

2

> *O ch'è cosa bella*
> *Andare in barca . . .*

I'll be my own fool,
Scaramouch is rogue enough to . . .
Anything, he'll join the Church of Scotland.

> *O guarda nel ciel*
> *Innumerabile stelle . . .*

Damn the stars, they get in people's way,
They make girls fall in love
With men that have no money,
They even make men think—a dirty trick,
Immoral, for a good man never thinks.
But I've a plan to thwart the stars;
We'll form a company, we'll buy the sky,
And let it out for advertising,
Large bills by day, electric signs at night;
We'll make a fortune and no one then
Will have a chance to think,
Because we'll have all houses made of glass—

Chi vuol esser lieto, sia;
Di doman non c'è certezza . . .
What's that?
A silly song made by a greasy Dago,
I can't pronounce his name.
Call him Lawrence Doctor.
Fancy a banker called 'Lorenzo',
A waiter's name, and singing songs like that;
My God! We have improved since then.

Ninetta è sol per Corilo,
Corilo per Ninetta;
Egli vivo e volubile,
Viva ella e legeretta . . .
Why do they go about like this at night
Strumming their silly mandolines
And bawling up and down the streets?
That's twice they've waked me up,
It'll spoil my stroke tomorrow.
Why don't the police interfere?
I'll make complaints and if it doesn't stop,
I'll . . . I'll go back to a decent country
Where a man can sleep
And get a game of tennis quietly.

O ch'è cosa bella . . .
Nights of Venice! Nights of Venice!
Drifting along the still canals of Venice
Hand-in-hand with Death—
She had red cherries in her hat.
Tintoretto strode along the walls
And Verdi swam with Chinese lanterns
Far out on the lagoon;
A thousand years of garbage underneath
And soft arpeggios overhead,

Drifting music, lips of lovers,
Stars in mist.

Break, break, my heart,
Flow down, my heavy tears,
For Gargamelle is dead
And all the world's too small to bury her.

> *'Twas Venice saw our true love's birth*
> *With soft Italian song and mirth,*
> *At Oberammergau—Herr Gott!—*
> *I loosed her tender virgin knot.*

Now lies she there . . .

3

We three set sail for Athens,
Mezzetin, the Conjuror and I.
Mezzetin had broken bail,
So we went with him,
Thinking we might persuade him to come back
And save our money.
But, as he pointed out, and we agreed,
Once they start raking in a man's affairs
God knows what they may find,
Arson, incest, theft, charity and beauty,
Most desperate crimes.

The voyage lasted such an age
That I got tired of playing cards
And went and sat upon the poop
And thought of Arethusa's azured arms.
The boat made no advance,
But the pointed seas kept running past,

Monotonous foam churned through the green;
I towed the sea-gulls on elastic threads.
Thinking of Arethusa turned me grave;
So first I made my will,
And then I thought I'd be an admiral
And call my bastard son Horatio;
Afterwards get divorced by going down to Brighton.

Then I was gently sick.

> *Ye mariners of England*
> *That harrow up the deep,*
> *O tell me is my own true love*
> *Adulterously asleep?*
>
> *How lovely are the Bournemouth bands*
> *That warble on the pier*
> *With here and there a Communist*
> *And here and there a peer.*
>
> *O willow, take me in your arms,*
> *O willow, give me peace,*
> *For I am chasing Byron's ghost*
> *Among the Isles of Greece.*

4

When we got to the Acropolis,
Mezzetin went off to buy some wine.

I wanted to sit down beside the Parthenon
And see the lizards on the broken steps,
And hear the wind among the columns,
Arcadian fluting, and look out to sea
To watch for Theseus's sail.
But the Conjuror was obdurate;

He would keep talking of Thucydides
And frightened me with all he knew of Pheidias;
I couldn't interrupt because he'd paid our fares.
Then he kept fanning with his bowler hat
And spouted French:

'O noblesse, O beauté simple et vraie! . . .
Les Scythes ont conquis le monde . . .
O Salpinx, clairon de la pensée . . .
Toi seule es jeune, toi seule es pure.'

I thought he had gone mad and told him so,
But he went on and on.

Penelope has spun a purple shroud
And scattered cypress on her marriage-bed.

Take up his bones, O lift them tenderly,
For they are brittle from the flame,
And brittle was his heart.

O wrap his bones in purple
For a King lies dead
And will not come again.

O tread upon the violet and the rose,
Lay waste the hyacinths among the rocks;
He will not come again.

O break the silver trumpet and the lyre,
Sully the marble, cut the crispèd bronze.
Byron is dead.

5

What's that to me?
My old friend Smut is dead.
He made a million out of pork
And sweated bawdy-houses.
Rest his soul;
His body lies within the abbey garth.

6

The Conjuror went on and on;
I thought he'd never stop quotation,
He seemed in such a frenzy;
I recognised Maurras and Tennyson
And heaven knows whom besides.
All at once he stopped,
Clutched me by a waistcoat button,
Shut his eyes and droned out this:

Telemachus grew old and drooled by the fire in the evening,
Paddling with palsied hands in the open breasts of his women
And wetting his oily beard in the wine-cup bossy and golden;
Red embers fell to grey as he mused of the ending of mortals,
The dying groans and the stillness, the funeral fire and the ash.

And he thought how his father Odysseus fared shipborne far
to the Westward
And came to the dwelling of ghosts and spake with the heroes
of Troy.
Now fain would Telemachus meet with the ghost of his father
Odysseus
To learn the state of the dead, if at last the soul be at peace.

Telemachus rose from his hall and builded a ship most stately,
Pitched it within and without and laboured the prow and the
  rigging;
Chose him an hundred feres and stepped up the mast; and with
  shouting
They threshed the sea with their oars and the long ship toiled
  through the waves,
Past the Isle of Calypso and past the land of the lotus
To the dark Cimmerian skies where alone hath Phœbus no
  glory.
In night, under night, through night, they traversed the death-
  dark ocean
Till softly the wet keel struck the sand of a silent shore.

There Telemachus builded three altars and digged them about
  with ditches
That the hungry ghosts might drink the speech-giving blood
  of the bulls,
That the ghost of father Odysseus might speak to his son of
  the dead.
Now thrice the length of a day they abode in that mortal
  darkness,
And thrice on the darksome soil the victims bled from the
  sword,
And thrice Telemachus cried the name of his father Odysseus . . .

But there came no hungry ghosts to lap up the blood from the
  ditches,
There came no sight and no sound, only infinite darkness and
  silence.

Mezzetin came sweating
And yo-ho-ing up the hill,
So burdened with his parcels and his bottles
That he banged his mandoline against the Propylæa
And swore Italian oaths.
He'd bought a pair of horn-rimmed spectacles,
Six litres of white wine and two of red,
And pounds of olives, bread and sausages,
And several heads of garlic.

We had a merry picnic,
Drinking from the wine-flasks
And all talking with our mouths full.

Now came still evening on . . .

The pure Athenian air grew dark
Like violet wine that drop by drop
Tints a clear pool.

A rigid dragon-fly sank moaning in the sea.

The Conjuror threw away his hat
Which changed into a hedgehog and ran off.
Mezzetin looked like a shadowy owl;
Grape-clusters sprouted round his head,
He strummed his mandoline . . .

> *O Evening Star,*
> *You bring back all good things*
> *The morning stole away . . .*

The Evening Star that Sappho saw
And Shelley after Plato sang

Droops over London like a tattered flower;
Incense of petrol and of burning coal
Rises to the thrones of heaven,
Sniffed and snuffled by ungrateful gods.

Pursued by angry bishops out of breath,
The lovers kiss and murmur on the grass,
Defying vermin sacred or terrene.
The star that smiles upon the Parthenon
Glares over London like a carbuncle . . .

Nine million hearts beat on to Kensal Green.

> *O Evening Star,*
> *You bring the Evening News,*
> *You bring the tired business man*
> *Back to his tired spouse;*
> *Sappho and Shelley you no longer bring.*

8

The moon rose out of Asia—
Anadyomene from the sea.
She wrung the water from her streaming hair;
It trickled down her moving flanks
Dripped from her breast-tips
And her knees.
The shining water splashed about our heads
And washed the Parthenon in silver;
Where it splashed and dripped and trickled
Everything grew splendid; all the rest was dark.
But it poured and flooded over Athens,
Drowned the houses in its pools,
Lapped swiftly up the hills
And rose about the citadel
Till we were gasping in a flood of moonlight,

Dashing it from flour-white faces
And swimming far above the Parthenon.
After we were drowned
And the coroner had sat upon our bodies,
We rose again,
And found our picnic place
Beneath the Parthenon.

Mezzetin shook the moonlight from his strings
And swayed and nodded as his fingers madly
    twitched;
Swarms of silver wasps flew upwards
With a buzzing of metallic wings,
Here and there a crimson butterfly
Rose and floated through the heavy air,
Then swooped down and settled on my heart.

Mezzetin sang scraps of foolish verse
But their core, their core was bitter,
Pungent to the mouth like pepper.

Now the Conjuror is something of a prig;
He reads too many books
And writes for reputable journals;
He hopes that some day the Academy
(The British one) will make his name immortal.
He got quite angry
And his face
Glowed like a parboiled meteor in the gloom:
He shouted: 'You're a lunatic; shut up'.

    Oh, we came up to Camden Town
      A-riding in a bus,
    And Solomon the Israelite
      Politely came with us.

He hired a hundred char-à-bancs
    To take his concubines and boxes,
And told us with a charming smile
    That they were grapes and we were foxes.

But they whistled the p'lice of Camden Town
    And Solomon got took up,
Trismyriagamy was the charge . . .

But there the Conjuror cut him short:
'You're drunk, you bloody fool,
Your nonsense makes me ill'.

Now I like Mezzetin;
Of course he sings most awful rot
And plays his mandoline too much;
But anyone can see that he's a fool,
And such a bitter fool.
So I thought I'd take the Conjuror down a peg.
I bawled into his ear:

'Let Mezzetin alone, he's my fool,
And he's not a bore like you.
At any rate his stuff's original,
Not watered William Morris dashed with Swin-
    burne
Like all your drivel about Telemachus'.
I thought he meant to kick me;
Instead he gave a frightful groan
And wept into his fingers.

So we finished up the wine in silence.

Things became a little queerer
But the wine had made me brave,
And though the Parthenon kept swaying
And the distant Caryatides waved their arms,
Intuitively I knew they would not fall.

Mezzetin kept changing in the darkness.
Somehow he'd thrown off his clothes
And his shoulder-blades glowed white in the
    moon;
Round his head were heavy grapes and vine-
    leaves
And his large eyes shone beneath them
As he softly moved the strings.

The Conjuror was half asleep,
But he'd changed too;
He looked benevolent and wise,
Fat as a monstrous pear
All buttoned up in clericals.

Then I thought:
'Gaiety's a kind of homage,
So is Mezzetin's fooling,
Yet perhaps the Conjuror was right—
I should have kneeled down
To kiss this sacred earth.
But I hate such demonstrations,
So German and self-conscious.

'What was it that the Greeks had we have not?
Why do we romanticise about them?
Theophrastus gives the game away;
The men of Athens were as base as we,
As dull, as treacherous, as selfish.
Do we praise Pindar overmuch—
The Isaiah of the race-course?
Could we make poems of a mule-race?

'Those Tanagra figurines
Look calm and indolent and graceful
As Gauguin's Tahitians.
They were not tortured by their passions.

'There was something more in Greece
Than tradesmen-citizens and slaves
And graceful flower-crowned girls.
Did they truly reach that harmony we hear of,
Balance of thinker, athlete, artist?
Plato mistrusted the imagination;
Pindar's thoughts are *clichés*
Dressed in splendid robes of gold and purple;
Did the Olympic victors think?'

Mezzetin stopped playing and his eyes were veiled
    in sleep.
'Yet this Parthenon is harmony,
Science and beauty reconciled with health.
We have beauty that's diseased and wanton,
Art that plays with ugliness and fantasy,
Science heavy, technical and mystic,
Stupid health for some—the rest imperfect.

'Lacking harmony, art's a grotesque.
They took the heavy wine of the imagination

And tempered it with snow-clad science.
French art—ragoûts and absinthe.
We have Shakespeare—burn the juniper.
(Yet a Greek would belch at Sophocles.)

'Too soon this harmony disappeared;
Commerce and treachery within,
On one side Roman arms
On the other Eastern myths.
Demosthenes fades to Chrysostom,
Plato to Iamblicus,
Pindar to Gregory of Nazianzus:
Esurient Greeks.

'Mechanics have devoured our art—
Our poets are all journalists, clerks or school-
     masters—
Shakespeare's an ocean-liner,
Donne an aeroplane
Bumping mysteriously through dizzy clouds.
Our Parthenon's a Jew hotel.'

All was silent
The shrill grasshoppers were dead.
Harmoniously the stars grouped themselves about
     the moon.

'Could we slide back and forth through space
     and time?
Thirty-two feet per second—
Gravity—the music of the spheres—
Pythagoras discovered strange proportions—
(I must be nodding off to sleep).
What was I thinking? O yes, harmony.
That's our problem—make a synthesis,

Reconcile the Conjuror with Mezzetin,
Make Mezzetin sing poems instead of nonsense
And make the Conjuror love art and gaiety;
All three live physically like Gauguin's Tahitians.

'Then they'd send us missionaries.'

10

That made me think of Hell.

It was like a crematorium
Or rather a Kadaver-factory
Where every day
Millions of persons were consumed to smoke.

Out of ten thousand towering chimneys
Gushed black greasy smoke
That whitened to a cloud of banknotes.

On the cloud sat God the Tradesman
Playing at the pianola
'Onward, onward, Christian soldiers';
In an armchair sat his sporty son
Bleating about Newbury races,
And winking at the angels underneath.
By the throne stood policemen-lictors
Bearing fasces made of golf-clubs.

Miss and Mrs God were calling
In the new Rolls-Royce war-chariot
(Ninety cherubim power, self-starting)
On the Abrahams and Isaacs.

All the Dominations played on Remingtons:
'Glory, glory be to banking!'

All the Powers with Linotypes sang:
'Glory to the laws of commerce,
Praised be Taylor, noble Patriarch,
Praised be Henry Ford, the Prophet,
Praised be Adam Smith, the Saviour'.

All the angels drove to work in tanks.

Showers of wounded grouse fell at my feet.

Far above them all, the mystic symbol,
Made of dazzling electric lights,
Ran about the sky and changed its colours,
Wove its green and scarlet bubbles to the message:
'More and more and more for ever,
Holy, Blessed, Glorious Mass Production'.

11

Mezzetin threw out a coil of melody
By which I clambered back from Hell.
I saw that Hell is the consequence of the hellish
    mind
And that anyone who will risk his life
Can escape from Hell.
It is useless to denounce the hellish mind
And no one yet has quite explained it.
Moreover, Hell is sometimes useful
If only to reveal its opposite.
If Hell disappeared we might disappear with it.
Perhaps Hell is the only reality
And we are its parasites?

'On Earth we are to enact Hell'.
Why?

On Earth it is better to enact Earth;
We must be men before we're gods or devils.

12

The Laconian said:
'O King,
Poverty is the faithful friend of Greece;
Virtue goes with her,
Daughter of wisdom and good government'.

13

Praise and a crown of glory to the race
Which first shall say: 'We have enough,
Bread, olives, meat, a little wine,
Rough wool dyed purple for our robes;
Now let us live as men'.

14

The Conjuror by now was fast asleep.
Mezzetin came nearer to me
And began whispering about Virgil.
All was so hushed on that high rock,
So motionless in still, pure light,
His muffled voice rang loud against my ears.

'Take the sixth eclogue,' he was saying,
'There you have harmony,
Science and myth, charm and austere truth,
Taste, imagination, and a flow
Of verse that holds the heart with beauty,
No need to dwell upon the symbolism—
Silenus, the Satyrs and the fairest of the Nymphs—
You know its meaning;
But observe how poetry obeys the laws of science,

How science sways to the rule of poetry.
Not a trace of arid Deism, no metaphysics;
Natural forces and the plastic sense.
Their world was clear and reasonable,
Yet not excluding beauty.
Not for them cowardly wails at death,
But the Evening Star at last
Shone out above Olympus.'

15

So he muttered in my ear,
And half from boredom, half from sleep,
I nodded slow assent.

Then I woke up:
'Saint Paul preached to the Athenians . . .
Why try to convince another?
Better to understand him and be silent,
Weigh if his truth relates to yours.
I hate these absolute convictions;
What are they but fanaticism?
Your harmony indeed is perfect
But perfection implies intolerance
For all that's not itself.
We are too nervous, too impatient,
Too inconsistent (if you will),
To seek or hold perfection;
What we build today we smash tomorrow.

'Stability, perfection, harmony—
Words that have no meaning for us,
Or a far-off, sentimental sound
Like waltzes of the 'eighties.
We look at all things curiously
And cling to and believe in none,

Not even in ourselves, least of all ourselves.
Inconsistency's our virtue,
Uncertainty our creed,
Eclecticism our taste;
Don't try to hold us down to anything,
Not even to inconsistency.

'Few have loved Athens more than we—
The pure clear light of Attic thought—
But do not think we always hate New York and
    London.

'I am compact of whims,
A fellow of the strangest mind'.

He murmured: 'Aguecheek'.

16

Mezzetin played rag-time on a banjo,
Clog-danced round the sleeping Conjuror;
Then he nasally orated:
'Ladies and gentlemen, fellow-citizens,
This is the famous Parthenon,
The greatest Temple in the World,
Built five thousand years B.C.
By Marcus Aurelius and Pericles
In honour of the heathen idol, Pallas Athene.
Although considerably out-of-date and dilapi-
    dated
It has been bought for ten million dollars
By a syndicate of our most cultured business-
    men.
Repairs and alterations will be rushed,
And in three weeks this old building
Will be as large and weather-proof

As the Capitol at Washington, D.C.
This, ladies and gentlemen, fellow-citizens,
Is another proof of the hearty co-operation
And goodwill of the New World to old Eurrup.'

> *O Pall Athena*
> *Amurica lo-oves you,*
> *O Pall Athena*
> *Here's a han' to you-ou*
> *Hoodle-hoo, hoodle-hoo.*
> *Our biggest high-brows*
> *Are nuts on culture,*
> *An' our Co-eds are*
> *Readin' Homer through,*
>   *Toodle-oo, toodle-oo,*
> *Our millionaires are buyin' Euri-pydes too*
>   *Hoodle-hoo, hoodle-hoo,*
> *And down in Boston where they bake the beans*
> *They know what Happapappazouglos means,*
> *So Pall Athena*
> *Here's a han' to you*
>   *Hoo-hoo-hoo-hoo.*

17

Strident, menacing, awful,
An owl hooted from the death-still temple,
And the earth shook beneath a mighty tread.
Mezzetin crouched low in terror
And the hair rose stiff upon my flesh;
A tall helmed figure strode between the pillars,
The moonlight flashed from gold and ivory
And the dreadful head burned from the seven-
   fold shield.
Then once more all was still,
And we trembled in the silence.

O pour un moment
que je laisse couler
tout le flot de ma (si belle!) amertume
que je bénisse la Mort
libératrice bénigne havre fleur du néant
apaisement
à quoi bon se démener?
les hommes sont grossiers les femmes grosses
m'écœurent je suis foutu
je déteste mes semblables
un chrétien me fait l'effet d'un gentil squale
les femmes que j'ai aimées
sont des squelettes peu aimables
voyez le coq qui monte la poule
et vous mangez des œufs
est-ce assez sale l'amour
on me fait voir un avenir sérieux
des avantages considerables
mais c'est ton ombre que je cherche
j'ai enterré cette femme
cependant tous mes pleurs se sont séchés
mais il ne s'agit pas de ça
je veux chanter les délices de la Mort
c'est dans un sépulcre fastueux
que je veux goûter mes délices
comme Voltaire à Genève
pensez donc on peut s'y ennuyer en seigneur
per omnia saecula saeculorum
j'ai ma réponse toute faite
pour le Jugement dernier
au moment où les anges du Seigneur
viendront braire dans mes oreilles pourries
je leur flanquerai un bon coup au cul

de mes pieds osseux
d'une voix caverneuse je hurlerai
'Chiens savants de l'Eternel
voulez-vous bien me foutre la paix?'

ainsi je compte achever mes vacances d'infini.

19

I have worn all servitudes,
Have drunk all shames.

Sometimes the cruel humour of the gods
Exasperates our slavish sycophancy;
But we shall never be revenged.

When we tear down their last bright curtain
We shall find nothing there.

They play with loaded dice
And when we find it out
And draw upon them—
Lo! They are not.

20

The Conjuror awoke and rubbed his eyes,
Then asked us why we were cowering there.
When we told him, he only laughed
And wagged a fat forefinger at us:
'Superstition! Superstition!
Your minds are broken mirrors
And you see the world in inchoate fragments;
You startle at a thousand false reflections,
Children, children!'

Then he seized a wrist of each of us
And dragged us terror-stricken up the steps
Into the tomb-like temple.
There was nothing except darkness
And a smell of dust and violets;
Fearfully I peered about
Dreading, hoping to see the frowning Goddess
Or the monstrous hooting owl.

Nothing,
Nothing in the darkness but our breathing
And the heavy silhouettes of pillars
And the dusty faint smell of violets.

I prayed:

> 'O Pallas,
> Guardian of the city,
> Sovereign of this most holy land,
> Surpassing all in war, in poetry, in strength,
> Be with us now
> And bring with you Victory—
> Clanging down to us on brazen plumes—
> Our friend in strife and battles,
> Appear to us now;
> Now, if ever, must you grant us victory,
> Pallas, O Pallas.'

Nothing,
Nothing in the darkness but our breathing
And the heavy silhouettes of pillars
And the dusty faint smell of violets.

21

The Conjuror broke the silence
And his voice grated in the gloom;

'What are these myths but half-truths, quarter-
    truths,
Dreams of semi-barbarous children
With an exquisite æsthetic tact?
Art is primitive and precedes true knowledge;
The Cro-Magnon, the Cretan, the Ionian
Possessed a subtle art-sense,
But their minds stumbled through crude cosmo-
    gonies.
The glory of Hellas is her thinkers,
Not her poets and her artists;
Other races have produced as great an art——'

(Mezzetin dropped his mandoline with a crash.)

'——But Hellas is the mother of science,
Praise then to Pheidias and Sophocles,
But glory, immortal glory, reverence,
To Thales and Pythagoras, Empedocles,
Parmenides and Heraclitus, Aristotle!'

Then he panted, out of breath with shouting.

Mezzetin whispered in my ear:
'Not a word, you note, of Plato;
Ask him what he thinks of *Phædrus*'.

I whispered back:
'He'd say Plato was a sophist and a poet
In all the mystic dialogues;
The man's an Aristotelian'.

Then aloud:
'When Greek science faltered
Into pedantry and futile subtleties,
Art remained.'

But the Conjuror grasped my arm and shouted:
'It became an art of death,
A stimulus to perverse and jaded senses;
Look!'

At his word a large flat disc of light,
Like Saturn's ring, circled the Parthenon,
Just level with the floor.
On the disc were monstrous visions of lust,
Suetonian bestialities, Caprean orgies, Spintrian
    chains;
There in bronze or marble in the moonlight,
Gleamed incestuous Myrrha and her guilty sire,
The bestial loves of Leda and Pasiphaë;
Ithyphallic satyrs reeling drunk
Plunged after panting Hyades;
There were Pan and Daphnis, the goat-group
    from Naples,
Salmacis and the Lesbian Sappho . . .
Greek myths made tangible for sensual Rome.

The Conjuror shook my arm:
'That orgy of the senses,
That bestiality, that vice—
There is Art uncontrolled by Science,
By love of truth and goodness.'
But I answered coldly:
'The renouncing of all limit is itself a truth.
This boundless orgy, this release of the senses,
This wine-drenched ecstasy,
These Priapic monsters,
Are but a type and figure of human life,
The sensual needs that hold us to the earth.
Even these wildest and most perverse excesses
Are disciplined by a sense of beauty;

Here is no sordid dread of sin,
No Anglo-Saxon cold vulgarity.
Trust me, the pagan orgy had its meaning
And that was, human life.
Despise the senses—even their temporary excess—
And science becomes a vain and arid thing,
A mass of quirks and symbols signifying nothing.
Crush the senses, they take terrible revenge
And waste men's lives, destroy even the earth's
    beauty.
I do not shrink from those mad orgies;
Share them I cannot,
For I am barred from them
By iron habits of race and training;
Neither do I condemn them, but observe.'

The Conjuror threw up his arms with a shriek:
'*Shemah Israel!*'
In a flash all vanished;
Mezzetin and I trembled in blank darkness.

22

Gradually a gleam of half-veiled starlight
Soaked the heavy blackness;
I saw the Parthenon had vanished,
Felt dry sand beneath my boots.

I was dizzy and my head ached;
I wondered stupidly at what had happened
And a weight of crime lay on me.
I wished I had gone to Athens care of Cook,
For under his large and brooding wings
The timid tourist is sheltered from all surprise.

I could scarcely see the others in the darkness,

But their eyes shone cat-like and oppressive,
Filling me with superstitious gloom.

All that followed is confused,
Blind and wandering like a nightmare,
Uneasy and interminable.

Sometimes one, sometimes the other
Led me by the arm.
We stumbled across a harsh desert
Where the night was loud with rustling wings;
Anubis yelped behind us,
Serpents slid beneath our feet;
We heard the pad of Sphynxes on the sand.

Then we wandered for another century
Through winding earthy passages
Cut with innumerable graves.
When my arm was held by Mezzetin
I heard sounds of distant singing,
Monotonous and poignant,
White-veiled women walked beside me
And I was touched to tears by a strange suavity
Compact of resignation, hushed desire,
And eager hope for some unknown good.

But when the Conjuror led me
The gloom raged with contending voices
And the clash of steel,
Dull flames glowed in the distance;
All was misery and confusion.

I hate to remember this long pilgrimage,
This horrible journey underground
Where we seemed imprisoned in the grave.

At length the darkness lightened;
The roof rose to a round arch,
That in turn soared upwards to a vault
And then we stood beneath a dome,
The mightiest in the world.
Long galleries and naves
Ran off in all directions,
And innumerable silent figures
Prayed or wandered through the twilight.

This vast and murmuring crowd
Was turned in one direction
Where on twisted columns of wrought bronze
Sat a cold and mitred god of porphyry,
Grasping in one hand a curious rod.

Knights and women, merchants, ploughmen,
   sailors,
All in strange and coloured garments,
Pressed forward to the rigid statue
And cast ringing money at its feet.

I could feel that Mezzetin was moved
And would have borrowed from me
A shilling for the idol;
But the Conjuror leaned towards me:
'Why do you keep craning round,
Scanning all these passing faces?
Whom are you looking for?'

I replied: 'Lorenzo Valla'.

Hardly had I formed the syllables
When we stood beneath a sunny sky,
Breathing air that had no smell of graves.

23

We were on a hill in some northern country;
From the absence of hedges and game,
The neatness of the distant fields
And one tree-lined road straight as a poker,
I concluded we were in France.
After those centuries of subterranean wandering
And the stifling incense-polluted air
I felt weary and exasperated.
I threw myself angrily upon the ground
And they stood gazing at me
With open mouths and hanging arms.
(Mezzetin, you will remember,
Lost his mandoline in the Parthenon
While I was arguing with the Conjuror.)

I felt so angry with the Conjuror
Because I thought he'd spoiled our trip.
So I attacked him:
'What right have you to spoil our holiday
Simply because you paid our fares?
You knew I wanted to be happy
And make fun of solemnities with Mezzetin.
He was as gay and silly as I could wish
Until your influence began to work.
Then he got quite didactic
And inspired me with solemn useless reveries.
How can we live like Greeks when we're not
    Greeks?
What's the use of trying to write like Virgil?
We can't create his sort of beauty
As well as he could, and I hate *pastiches;*
We must live our own way,
Write like ourselves, not Virgil—
Here I am arguing again! It's all your fault;

And never in my life before
Have I passed through such lugubrious moods
As you've inspired in me.
When I said I wanted a fool,
I meant a merry fool, not two solemn ones.
I loathe all argument and preaching;
Why don't you go away and leave me?'

But the Conjuror replied impressively:
'You can leave us but we cannot leave you
Until you drive us from you;
If we go, we go for ever.
Mezzetin and I are enemies——'
(Here he scowled like Huxley's bust.)
'We were once friends
That's why we hate each other now.
I know you thought you could reconcile us,
But you can't; you've got to choose;
One of us you can keep
Or you can send us both away.
You know what we stand for; choose.'

I was abashed at this, but answered:
'Look here, when we started out
I was full of gaiety and high spirits,
Ready to take the world and life as jests
And laugh at them with Mezzetin;
But you've destroyed my *verve*
And I'm as dull and solemn as a tired reviewer.
It's true I like Mezzetin more than you,
But one can't spend life only in mocking dullards
Or even in gaiety and music;
One must have something positive
And that you seem to give me.
If I lose one of you, I'm incomplete;

If both, it's mental death.
Others have reconciled you, why not I?
At any rate, I won't choose yet;
Sit down and rest a little here,
And you shall take us on our next adventure.'
Without a word, they sat beside me;
All three of us chewed our bitter-sweet cud,
And mine was mostly bitter.

24

O miserable condition of humanity,
Coming from nothing, into nothing going,
Striving with princes and with powers for
    nothing.
Who indeed would sweat and fardels bear for
    nothing?
What's a man?
Fortuitous concurrence of whirling electrons,
A problem in mathematics and physics;
Or a divine soul sheathed in clumsy mud
Striving towards God?
We cheat ourselves with words
And only think we think,
Either in terms which analysed mean nothing
Or in terms made arbitrarily exact.
What is Reality?
We start from ourselves,
We return to ourselves;
Each inhabits a narrow chrysalis
He calls reality because it fits his logic;
Outside his universe is the expanse of
    mystery.
Why should the universe be rational?
Why should we say:
It must fit such and such a rule?

That way madness lies and—
Damn my primitive metaphysics.

When we're young, in love, and the sun shines,
Life is delicious; some exuberant force
Plays through our veins,
Everything delights us, all is beauty.
So at twenty, I beheld the Gulf of Naples;
All my being towered into a splendid flame—
Sunlight sparkled on the sea
Odysseus cut with carven prow,
And the sirens still were singing.
Every rock-cleft blossomed with narcissus,
Every slope with broom and vine and lemon;
Every hill was sacred to a goddess.
When what mortals call the morning mist
Swept in bright procession from the sea,
I beheld the daughters of the ocean,
Heard their clear song through the scented air.
Noon was filled with voices,
Not alone cicadas,
But echoing calls of fauns and dryads
Happy in flower-sweet recesses.
Evening came and like a noble woman
Came the heavenly moon and round her
Glowed the large and silent stars . . .

Pallid stammering words!
Had I died then life were perfect.
Bitter, bitter-true the saying:
'Whom the gods love dies in youth'.
And the gods who loved me sent me Death;
Many months I walked beside her,
Often tempted by her sweet embraces,
Often knowing that a step would make me

Once again that splendid towering flame.
Yes, the gods were kind, but I was cowardly.
Thrice Death clutched me, thrice my will re-
   pelled her;
Then the gods abandoned me.

We grow old, the sun grows tarnished;
Life becomes an autumn twilight;
From a lifeless sky rain settles,
Drips from drooping boughs and trickles
Noiselessly from slates and dreary walls. . . .

When the flame goes, man's a husk, a ghost,
Herding miserably with other ghosts,
Sunk in apathy or shrieking at his memories.
That is Dante's 'maggior dolore'.

25

What's to do then?
For to lament is pitiful,
Most unbecoming men who strove with Haig.

First, the bare bodkin, which perhaps is best;
Then art, religion, science;
Delightful games when played with gusto;
Then the moral philosophy of the ancients—
Plato or Aristotle, Zeno or Epicurus;
Take your choice or take them all
And build a fine new chaos . . .

   While Phrygian shepherds watched their flocks
   All seated in a mead,
   The eagle of the Lord came down
   And bore off Ganymede.

My own ideals are plenty of fishing and rag-
    time;
I love to feel a fat chub on my hook
Although his carcase dismays and bothers me,
And then that heavenly rag-time:

> '*Are you from Dixie?*
> *Yes, I'm from Dixie!*
> *Well, I'm from Dixie too-oo-oo!*'

Gorgeous, isn't it?
Such a change from Beethoven and Sousa.
And the joy of dancing to it with a pure, bright
    girl—

> *There's a hole in her stocking . . .*

I've sometimes thought I'd be an *artist;*
I'm told they make a *lot* of money,
Not a cubist, of course, but a *real* artist,
Like old Sir Humpty-Dumpty. . . .

But no, there's no solution;
Better go on as before;
Thank God there's no encore after the last
    curtain.

So carry on, Sergeant-Major, carry on.

26
I spoke the last words aloud
And they roused the Conjuror from sleep;
For it was night again.

He stood up and said:
'Get your rifles, men, and come along'.

Mechanically I arose and found my rifle,
Shook my pack and stood by Mezzetin,
Thinking: 'O my God, it's this misery again;
I've often thought I'd wake up from a dream
And find that we were back in it;
Well, it's no sillier than all the rest,
But the slavery of it's dreary.'

It appeared that Mezzetin and I were privates,
But the Conjuror (of course) was Sergeant-
  Major.
Off we went, to the music of night-firing,
The pleasant evening hymn of Lewis guns
And the pretty fire-works from the line.
The Conjuror led us down a sunken road,
Along the duck-boards of a trench—
As usual I caught my bayonet in wires,
Bashed my iron hat against a bridge
And wrenched my ankles on sixteen broken
  duck-boards.
At last we reached the front line;
A quiet relief—only two men hit.

The Conjuror bustled up and down,
Talking to officers and placing sentries;
Mezzetin and I hopped off,
Nipped into the signallers' dug-out,
And plotted how to steal the sergeants' rum.
But the Conjuror discovered us and said:
'I want you men to come with me;
I'm going on patrol.'
Mezzetin and I gazed wildly at each other;

I thought: 'Now I know this isn't true—
A Sergeant-Major on patrol!
It must be some dreadful nightmare.'
We went crawling out; the usual thing—
Shell-holes, puddles, sand-bags, knife-rests,
The regulation ration of skeletons, Mark VI.
All went well until we reached their wire;
I could see Mezzetin ahead of me
Caught on a rusty picket festooned with spikes,
Swearing in whispers like a perfect gentleman.
Then that damned Conjuror exclaimed:
'Look out! I see a Boche!'
Fired his revolver at a stump.
Of course I rolled into the nearest shell-hole;
Up went the Verey lights, down came minnies,
Rifle-bombs, grenades, rifle-fire,
And a beautiful scherzando of machine-guns.
Gradually the concert quieted down;
Suddenly I thought of Mezzetin
And knew he must be dead.
My heart went icy; I felt sick, sick,
And something vital left me for ever.

Then I knew that Mezzetin
Was as much to me as life itself;
I wished a bomb would fall into my shell-hole,
For I felt too numb to stand up to the bullets.

> *Who should remember you if we forget?*
> *Those who lift top-hats and lay down wreaths?*
> *Or those who buried you, dry-eyed and lousy?*

The Conjuror crawled over to my shell-hole.
'Where's Mezzetin?'
'Why, dead, of course, what made you fire?'

229

'Where's his body?'
'Over by that picket, I suppose.'
He stood straight up; I whispered:
'Lie down, lie down, you'll draw their fire'.

Then I noticed a peculiar silence;
Not a gun, a shot, a light;
All was sinister and still.
I climbed from the shell-hole
And we walked towards Mezzetin.
There he lay, dead, dead, in mud and blood.
The Conjuror rolled him over, felt his heart:
'Yes, he's dead right enough.'
Then to my disgust and anguish,
He kicked the passive body, muttering:
'I'm glad he's dead;
I always hated and despised him,
With his eternal jangling mandoline
And stupid jokes at high and serious things;
Now he's gone, we'll make a man of you.'

I was aghast and trembling with rage.
Of course I know I should have killed him then,
But I always was a coward
And never could face the horror
Of jabbing a bayonet in a man's belly;
And as usual, my rifle was unloaded.
All I could do was gasp:
'You murderer, you murderer.'

27

Here of course should come an elegy on Mezzetin;
But now he's dead I have no interest in writing.
Instead, I'll give you his obituary news.

On a wooden cross in France: 'R.I.P.
012342 Private Mezzetin. 1/7 Fool's Brigade.
Killed in Action. 1st April, 1917.'
In the 'List of Casualties':
The same, minus R.I.P.
In the 'List of Recent Wills':
'Sir Hanley Podge, broker, wholesale provision
    dealer,
Receiver of stolen goods, £1,325,498.
Mezzetin (the famous clown) £1.10 in silver'.

28

Logically, the story ends with Mezzetin's death,
And if it's bored you hitherto,
Think how bored you'll be now Mezzetin is
    dead.
But life is seldom logical;
It flows on and on and on,
Growing a little dingier every year,
Until it peters out in some inglorious wise.
Mine isn't over yet,
But I must bring this story down to date
As rapidly as possible;
But it's dull, it's dull, it's dull.

29

Somehow we drifted back to London.
The Conjuror was quite concerned about me
And even he could see that I was melancholy.
Sometimes he clapped me on the back (a thing
    I hate)
And cried with hearty cheerfulness (which I
    loathe,
Because it's humbug, an accepted cheat),

'Cheer up, my son, we'll make a man of you,
Now Mezzetin is dead'.

And I would think:
'Yes, and you're his murderer'.

As I mooned about incapably,
Living extravagantly on my blood-money,
The Conjuror grew more concerned:
'Come, you must rouse yourself and act;
Introduce me to your friends'.
I replied: 'I haven't any friends,
But I know lots of people'.
So we went to parties.
Some people said to me: 'How well you look,
Quite manly and set up. Your gratuity
Will come in useful to start you in life'.
Others said: 'Why do you look so odd?
You seem almost demented with misery'.
I always said the same thing in reply:
'Of course, I'm radiantly happy;
Who wouldn't be with all you clever people?
But I'm ambitious;
I want to shoot nine politicians,
Fourteen titled tradesmen, two colonels,
—One general and a Sergeant-Major'.
Then naturally they giggled and the women
    said:
'Oh, *isn't* he too silly?'

The Conjuror was very strong on knowledge.
He got me a ticket for the British Museum
And made me go there with him
While he did his 'work'—
Thus he pompously described it.

Work! Drivel for the newspapers—
Gagged, except to bawl or simper lies.

You couldn't even smoke there;
So I sat and yawned and dawdled,
Watched the brisk discharge of volumes
From the forty miles of magazine.
Ennui of knowledge without wisdom
Soaked into my flesh and numbed me.
The Conjuror read on and scribbled,
While I thought of Mezzetin or nothing.

30

Once we met a wealthy tradesman,
Strong and cruel as an Assyrian King.
The Conjuror said something about soldiers'
    hardships;
But the rich man caught him up:
'Hardships? We had hardships, too, in England.
One winter—can it be believed?—the govern-
    ment
Rationed my coal, allowed me only one ton a
    week,
Coal from my own mines too.'

I felt so sorry, so indignant.
Only one ton a week, and from his own mines
    too!
I felt I'd like to overthrow a government
Capable of such injustice;
And I blushed deeply at the Conjuror's frightful
    gaffe.

31

To avoid all this I slept by day
And walked about the streets at night;
But the Conjuror came with me,
Gave me good advice unquenchable.
I felt sure there was something I ought to do,
Something rather sudden and bloody,
But what it was I could not think.
Political assassination I rejected—
Useless to cut off one Hydra-head;
Anarchist attacks—futile and cruel;
Bolshevism—a silly tyranny;
Some inbred scepticism destroyed all my plans.
So I walked about the streets at night.

London before dawn is not uninteresting,
A city given up to sleep and criminals
And slow policemen;
But it's flat and ugly, tiring.
Sometimes as we tramped about
And the Conjuror discoursed intently,
I would think, to put him out of mind:
Behind those dismal house-fronts
Lies a honeycomb of silent cells;
All is motionless, frozen to a seeming death,
Arranged for God to brood over.
There are the boxes for tomorrow's letters,
There sit the typewriters, untouched, in covers,
There lie the files, the tabulated documents,
There are the cleared desks and the minutes
Of yesterday's Board Meeting, rigid, passive;
There are the women's shop-fronts
With their hats and dresses, foolish gew-gaws,
Limp and colourless and lifeless,

Lighted strangely by the street-lamps;
There are the empty restaurant windows,
There the jewellers', barred and shuttered,
There the reeking taverns, dark and hostile.

Time glides over them, but does not touch;
Stars peer grimly round the roof-tops;
A tree beside a lamp-post
Trembles with unnatural greenery;
The wood-blocks in the soundless streets
Gleam as if washed in slime;
Dust and dirty paper drift on sinister winds
That titter a ferocious irony
Or gasp a misery not fit for words . . .

Time glides over them, but does not touch;
Does not touch? Look closer, listen . . .
There a fissure opened in the brick-work,
There a broken fibre of wood creaked,
There a road-block tilted, oh so slightly,
But it tilted;
There old papers grew a little yellower,
Imperceptibly, but Time is patient.
There a spawn of fungus died,
But Time is patient,
Holds a myriad seeds within her bosom;
There a dead leaf fell, sank slowly
From the stately spreading plane-trees;
Time is patient.
Wrapped in shrouds of white,
Extended, couched athwart, uneasy,
Lie the million breathing corpses
In their dark funereal cells.

Now if God should speak?

Should plunge the houses
Fathoms deep in earth?

But Time is patient.

32
One morning about three o'clock,
Coming back past Waterloo,
We stopped upon the bridge
And I gazed into the water;
More listless and depressed than ever,
Thinking of Mezzetin and Captain Cook,
Dead dogs drifting out to sea,
And Nashe's Isle of Dogs,
And patata and patati . . .

By now, I'd come to hate the Conjuror,
But most of all his blatant, cheery voice,
So unconcerned with the tragedy of things,
So massively stupid, pyramidally ignorant,
A symbol of the non-perceptive mind—
A thing that makes you stamp with rage
Because it's iron-clad against your scorn,
Padded against the shock and stab of truth
With centuries of crusted humbugs.
There we stood; I brooded sulkily,
While he lacerated my nerves
By lending me a helping hand.
What he said I can't remember clearly;
Something about humanity and work,
And sacrifices not in vain,
And getting rid of foolish notions;
Then he quoted some insulting verses
With a lot of 'ifs' and ended
With his favourite piece of cant:

'We'll make a man of you, my son,
Now Mezzetin is dead'.

This was more than I could bear;
Exasperation lent me wits;
At last I saw what I had to do.
Rapidly I stooped,
Seized him firmly by the ankles,
And, despite his squeals and clutchings,
Splashed him headlong in the river,
Down among the dead dogs and the Roman
    coins.

I watched the whirlpool disappear,
(They never found his body),
Then walked calmly to my room,
Giving each policeman a virtuous good night,
Went to bed and slept a heavy sleep . . .

33

Every morning now at half-past seven
Ethel thumps me in the back;
Up I leap, a loyal English husband,
—Whistle in the bathroom, gulp my bacon,
Kiss the children—John and James and Mary;
There's another coming, name not settled—
Buy the morning paper as I hasten to the tube
And read of all the wonders of the age.

At the office I am diligent and punctual,
Courteous, well-bred, and much respected;
Though the babies are a sad expense,
Every month I save a little money.
Every evening Ethel greets me meekly:
'Tell me all your joys and sorrows, darling'.

Then I say how Mr Sludge reproved me
For a letter 'not at all in keeping
With this firm's high, honourable traditions';
Or how Mr Hopkinson reported
I deserved promotion for my willing service.
Everything I do is wise and orderly;
My will is made, my life's insured,
The house is being slowly purchased;
Yesterday I bought a family grave.

Yet,
Sometimes when my stalwart figure
Strides the bleak suburban golf-links;
Sometimes when I lie awake
(Too much coffee after dinner);
Memories of old adventures,
Pangs from the forgotten years,
Haunt me, wound me, tear my heart.
Need I fall so low as this?
Need I prison up my spirit
In so meek and regular a cage?
Had they lived, had I been different . . .

Though I quench such thoughts and think of
    Ethel,
Tell myself that I've been made a Man,
An Empire-Builder and a taxpayer;
Miserably mocking voices,
Elf-land flutings, tags of verses,
Scraps of song and distant laughter,
Tinkling of a ghostly mandoline,
Memories of Athens and of Naples,
Of a life once vowed to truth and beauty,
Pierce me till I start and gasp in anguish . . .

34

To the palace of the ancient King I come,
Leaning heavily upon my staff,
Singing one last song.

I am but a murmur of words,
I am but a dark vision,
A dream in the night.

O children and ye old men,
Lament for the birth of a babe;
Lead on, lead on to the bourn.

Farewell, mysterious earth,
Farewell, O sea,
Farewell, farewell.

Now for ever shall my lips be still
And for ever my hands be at rest.

I flatter no gods with prayer,
They are subject and mortal as we,
Crushed by inscrutable Fate.

Farewell, mysterious earth,
Farewell, impregnable sea,
Farewell,
Farewell.

A DREAM IN THE LUXEMBOURG

A DREAM IN THE LUXEMBOURG

FOR B.

Si vis amari, ama

1

THERE are plenty of people to despise the dreamer of day-
    dreams,
And I've a friend, a learned friend with a wistful smile,
Who calls it a disease we inherit from Rousseau,
But I doubt if the learned friend has ever been really in love—
Sleepless, eatless, let Rome in Tiber melt love.
But never mind him, let me tell you my day-dream,
For who can be in love, in Paris, in June,
And the lady of his thoughts in another country,
Without day-dreaming under the trees in the Luxembourg?

Now I am so much moved as I write this
That my hand shakes with excitement,
And there is so much to say
I scarcely know where and how to begin;
So hard is it to be truly Reasonable
When you are a little crazy with a Romantick love.

2

When I least expected it, the miracle happened,
For I saw a wood-nymph visibly seated before me
In the shape of a girl. . . .
And Love pierced me to the heart so that the wound still
    throbs.
But I mean it—that Eros of the Euripidean chorus,
That Amor you may read of in Catullus,
Had me in His power—that same Amor Peire Vidal saw

243

One spring morning riding through the fields of Provence—
And it is quite true, as the Ancients and the Romance poets
    knew,
That love is a sudden thing which stabs at the vitals
And leaves an ache like a wound in the left breast.
I was only near her for four days
And all that time my mind was in confusion,
For there were so many reasons why I should not love again,
And so many reasons why I should not love her.
So I fought against my love, trying to be 'honourable',
And I was so miserable and in such agony of mind
It was like the dark night of the spirit
Which the mystics know when their God abandons them.
But on the second day there came a moment when I ceased to
    struggle,
Let myself taste the happiness of being near her;
For a moment my eyes met hers, and for a moment
I gazed into the loveliest of human minds—
The water knew its God and blushed.
I was the water, and she was my God.
Then I saw that the Gods had brought me
A laughing tree-nymph, crisp-haired like the ilex,
With eyes that seem immortal.

I said to myself: This will cause me much agony,
For doubtless she will never love me—
What is one more lover to her
Who must have many lovers offering her devotion
And their peerless selves in exchange for her complaisance?
Doubtless she thinks me a lout or a fool
Because I am silent or stammer when she speaks to me.
But who shall strive against the Gods?

What is there in life that endures?
Why do we assume that love must last for ever?
Why can we not be wise like the Epicureans
Who thought not of possession but of enjoyment?
Is not a man a man, and a woman a woman?
If she loved me, should I mind that she has had lovers?
Are we Jews or Catholic bigots
Or—which is even worse—rich pious Methodists?
Did Epicurus love Leontion?
Did he not love Ternissa? Yes or No?
Was Lesbia so faithful to Catullus?
Well then? All we have's today.
Cras amet, if you can,
And if you really love once in a life,
Give thanks to all the Gods,
You'll not find love at every street-corner
Nor every drawing room either.

Yesterday I plucked out two grey hairs.
Memento mori. Yet a few more years,
And what remains of me and—hell!—of her?
Must fair women die?
I'll not believe it, Death is masculine.
Death, like a war-lord, wants more man-power,
And, by God, he gets it, I've seen him get it.

How many yellow dead men have I seen?
Carried how many stretchers?
Stood by how many graves—of young men, too?
Reported how many casualties?
But one gets used to it, quite used to it,
And it seems nothing for men to die,
Nothing for one to die oneself.

But for a fair woman to die,
And that a woman one loves or has loved—
No, it is incredible, they don't die,
They turn into the brightest flowers
Or become young graceful trees,
Or lovely white-winged sea-birds,
Or the lovelier fragile clouds
Poised like warm snow in the summer air.
Could not Alcestis and Admetus change their rôles?
After some happy weeks or months or years
What lover would refuse?
Of many murmured kisses give her the rich last,
Gaily take leave, and grasp the proffered hand
Of Hermes, Leader of the Dead,
Give her some twenty years you might have lived
A selfish, dwindling, middle-aged dull man,
And let her keep her youth,
And give her to a younger lover's arms,
Who, in his turn, shall give his life for hers!

I say she shall not die. . . .

4

It was five on a sunny afternoon,
And I sat on one of those uncomfortable iron chairs
Under the trees of the Luxembourg,
Rather apart from the crowd,
So that the passing people seemed like trees moving,
And the children playing, like graceful forest animals;
In the distance I could see the wavering fountain jet,
Always rising and always falling in foamy parabolas
Like the path of a comet fixed in tremulous water.
And all this I am trying to tell you
Is the day-dream which suddenly came to me

Quite unawares, as a poem springs up fountain-like
When one is not even thinking of a poem.
In an hour I lived through my dream,
And it was so vivid, so intense, that I saw and heard nothing
Of the people and the children and the trees and the sunlight,
But saw only my dream.
That is why I am telling it
As if it had really happened, and were not merely a dream;
And also because, like an incantation,
Desire put into words may control reality. . . .

5

For long months I had not seen her.

It was an April morning in England
With a cold north-westerly wind
And cold dark sleet-showers
Blotting out the uncertain spring sky.
I was sitting at my table writing a dull article,
When I saw the telegraph boy coming to the door,
And thought: what boring news does he bring?

My heart leaped when I saw it was from my love,
Who wired from a small seaside town in France:
'I am here at the Auberge des Deux Amants,
Would you like to meet me?'

In an instant my mind was made up—
For would I not go ten thousand miles
Only to look at her and to watch her living?—
So I took my pen and wrote:
'Starting immediately shall wire you again from Paris
My beautiful love I adore you.'
And the telegraph boy, who is friendly, said:

'It'll cost a lot, sir, threepence a word, sir'.
And I said: 'I don't care if it's a pound a word.
Take it back at once, and telephone to the garage
That I want a car here in half an hour'.

Then there was the inevitable scene
Of making excuses and arrangements and packing;
But my mind was working like a high-power engine
And I made no mistakes,
Even remembered to arrange for my letters,
And gave my address, American Express, Paris.

The tumult in my heart as I set off in the car;
(I could not wait for the slow country train.)
Why had she sent for me? A jest? Was she ill? In trouble?
A whim to see if I would leave everything,
Drop my pen in the middle of a sentence, a word,
And go to her because she had called me?
Perhaps I could stay near her for a week,
Perhaps even in the same hotel—
Perhaps we should go bathing together with her friends
(Who would they be, and should I like them?)
And perhaps, when I left, I should kiss her once,
For a kiss is not such a great thing
Even from a wood-nymph with crisp hair like a young
    ilex tree. . . .

First to the Bank to get money—
Qu'il est malheureux d'aimer sans une grande fortune!—
Then the express to London and the night express to Paris.
Not a wink did I sleep—for how can one sleep
As the great express hurtles over the lines
Too slowly, too slowly for one's rushing thoughts,
Bearing one nearer and nearer to one's love?
In a dream, in a dream of love I went to her,

Hoping for little, asking only to be near her,
Pleased with the rocking of the boat I usually dread,
Glad to see that we left the clouds behind in England
And that the stars looked clear and cheerful over France,
Pleased to be back in France, and not even angry with
    the Customs.
Paris—a taxi to the American Express to find train-times
And to arrange about letters,
Then another taxi to send her a telegram:
'Arriving five today,
Will go to another hotel and call this evening
Wildly happy I still adore you'.
Then a rush to buy her two or three trifles she likes—
She has only to say so once and I remember them—
And a final rush to the Gare d'Orléans.
'Only five hours and I shall see her,'
I thought, as the train started from Paris.
But do you know how long five hours can be
Even in an express on a sunny April day in France
When it is carrying you to meet a wood-nymph
Whom you love in a way which would horrify a bishop?
Somehow the hours and the stations passed.
At every station I wanted to send her a telegram,
But refrained, on account of the hotel servants.
The waiter in the restaurant car thought Monsieur
    was *maboul*,
For Monsieur scarcely ate any food,
And half-way through the meal stood up in the rocking train,
Drank one glass of the best wine available
And then abruptly left the table. . . .
If only I could tell you how happy I was
Through the long hours of that long journey,
If I could tell you the thoughts I thought,
And the hopes and the fears, and the tenderness,
The aching desires—for even a wood-nymph is half human

249

And one is very human oneself,
While Ovid will tell you how the daughters of gods
Have stooped to a mortal's couch.
But always in the end it came back to this:
'She has never said she loved me
And I do not think she does;
Yet it will be felicity to be near her,
For she cannot but feel she is beloved—
A fact which displeases few women—
Sometimes she will smile at me,
Even let me look into her eyes
(Why is that so poignant and so necessary?)
And let me hold her hand when no one is looking'.

At last the train slowed down for the last time
At the station of the town
From which she had wired me,
And I got down the high steps of the train
With my bag and a wild assortment of emotions,
Thinking: 'I will find a cab and tell the driver
To take me to the hotel nearest the Deux Amants. . . .'
At that moment I saw her standing on the platform,
So straight and trim in her neat spring dress
With the brim of her hat just wide enough and curved
    enough
To bring out the sweetness
As well as the gaiety in her face.
She laughed her whimsical laugh
As she saw my amazement, and held out her hand.
I loved her, I loved her, I loved her.
My heart gave a great leap, as it does
When a hidden gun unexpectedly bangs off
Two yards behind your head.

I could not speak, I could not speak one word;

Just dropped my bag, and kissed her hand,
For in France you may kiss the hand of a married woman.
She withdrew her hand, because I think people looked at us,
(No doubt it was rather a long kiss)
But she did so very gently.
And as I did so she let me look into her eyes,
And my heart—which was beating madly—
Gave another preposterous jump,
For never had she looked at me so kindly,
And I even thought there was a tenderness in her gaze.
'Come,' she said, 'I've a porter for your bag,
And a car waiting outside. I'll drive you along.'

Now, if you're the slow northern type that I am
You'll understand my happy confusion.
I was so bewildered
That my *esprit* hadn't even got on to the *escalier;*
I only said: 'That's dear of you',
And followed her along the platform.
She stopped at the telegraph office, saying:
'Wait a moment, I must send some telegrams'.

Outside the station was a new French two-seater,
And it seemed almost too much honour
That the porter should strap my shabby bag on the back,
And even more of an honour that I should sit in it
Beside my love.

As we started I said to her:
'It makes me quite happy to be near you;
How dear of you to ask me with your other friends.
But I'm so anxious about you.
You look beautiful and well,
But are you in any difficulty?
Can I do anything?'

251

She laughed again
(Do you know how sweet it is
To hear the soft laughter of one's love
With just a touch of mockery in it,
When she seems happy and looks so beautiful?)
And she said: 'No, nothing wrong;
Just that I am alone here
And thought I'd like a companion'.

Alone, alone! So we should be alone together,
And we could walk and eat and talk together,
And go on excursions and bathe together,
And she would read to me in her clear voice,
And we could argue about books and painting,
And talk scandal about all our friends
(If we wanted to do anything so silly)
And tell each other what we were writing and thinking.

Alone, alone with my love!
Then I noticed she had driven on to a road,
A warm southern country road
Leading straight out into the country,
And I said: 'Haven't you gone wrong?
Where are you taking me?
Which hotel are you taking me to?
Are they outside the town?'

Then once more she laughed,
And half bent forward over the steering wheel,
Saying: 'You're pretty mystified, aren't you?'
And I admitted I was mystified,
But I didn't mention the wild hope
Which had suddenly leaped up in me.
And she said: 'Shall I tell you now
Or will you wait for the surprise?'

And I answered: 'Please tell me now,
No surprise could make me happier.'

And so, as we drove along the country road
With the sea to our left
And a range of hills in front of us
And another range of hills to our right,
She told me, my love told me her 'surprise'.

'I've been here more than a month', she said,
'Writing, and I've rented a little country house
Close by the sea at Sainte Véronique,
Which is a little fishing village
At the end of that long promontory over there,
About ten miles from here,
And you're going to stay there with me—if you want—
Until one or both of us get tired.'

Here that infernal reticence came on me again,
(It's a damned shame to send boys
To those imbecile Public Schools
Which destroy all immediate response
And ability to conquer shyness,
In order to make obedient Empire-builders,
But thank God I always hated them and their sort,
And fought against them, blindly, but to the bitter end,)
So I couldn't say anything.
But after all there is a sort of a poet in me,
And that prompted me;
I put my left arm gently round her,
And she didn't mind at all, but let it stay.
'And you asked me to come!
How wonderful, how wonderful!
It's far more exciting
Than anything in the Arabian Nights. . . .'

'Don't be too flattered,' she said,
(But her smile was tender
And I didn't mind her teasing me,
For I suppose a wilful whimsical tree-nymph
Cannot help teasing a lover)
'Don't be too flattered,
You're only here to temper my solitude.
Yesterday morning I woke up
And decided I would have to have company—
Yes, a lover if you like.
I remembered there were three men in England
Who had all sworn they loved me,
You and B. and C.;
So I sent you all the same telegram.
I pretended to be staying at the Deux Amants
And arranged with them to send on telegrams.
I knew you were all in the country
About the same distance from London,
So you all had the same chance to get here together.
I decided that if you all arrived by the same train
I might give the preference to the one
Whose telegram got here first;
And if one of you was so ardent
As to get here before the others
I thought he might have a very good chance. . . .'

(I suddenly went cold, for I had forgotten
That there are airplanes between London and Paris,
And that I might have been beaten in the race.)

'But, of course,' she went on, to console me,
Thinking that the tightening of my arm
Meant that I was jealous, when it only meant
I was calling myself a fool for not taking an airplane,
'Of course, I hoped it would be you, and it was you.

B. wired that he frantically regretted delay
And hoped to be here within a fortnight—
And C. was even more gallant and particular,
He said that as soon as he had finished his picture—
Which he thought would be next Wednesday—
He would run up to town for a day or two
To pick up a few necessary things,
And then would come straight on here,
So you see, you won.
I wired them just now: "Too late".
I suppose you happened not to be doing anything?'

'I only left a word unfinished
In the middle of an unfinished sentence. . . .'

'Don't protest too much, I shan't believe you. . . .'
And at that moment we stopped at the gate
Of a short drive leading to a large cottage
Built, facing the sea, in the Italian style,
With balconies and a verandah and three large stone-pines,
And a run of broken ground down to the shore,
Which was a little cup of a bay
Almost at the end of the promontory. . . .

6

Here, for a moment, I must pause,
For, as you see, I've come to the core of my dream;
There is so much to tell
And I don't know what I ought or ought not to tell. . . .
And another thing troubles me about all this—
Did it really happen?
Was it only a dream in the Luxembourg?
Was it a vision of what will be,
My spirit brooding over her so intensely

That for an hour I saw the future?
For, though I know it all went on in my brain,
Yet it was so vivid I seemed to behold it
Clearly in a clear crystal glass.
I saw her and I saw myself.
And yet it all happened within myself.

I did not go into the garden, saying:
'I will sit down and tell myself a tale
Of what I should like to happen
And how she came to love me'.
But just after I had paid my *sous*
For the hard iron chair in the gardens,
Suddenly I was at my desk in England,
As I told you just now, and the dream unrolled
Exactly as I tell you with all the details
I remember so clearly and could not invent.
But what is the present, past and future?
If it did not happen, it will happen.
Oh, promise me it shall happen,
For when I assert that it must happen
Either now or in many millions of years,
I do not quite believe my assertion.

But you may think it far more amazing
That even in a dream a supple wood-nymph
Should love such a man.
Well, the Queen kissed Alain Chartier's lips
(And he was no beauty among *trouvères*)
And the Lady Marguerite,
Who was the fairest of all the ladies of Provence,
Loved Guilhem de Cabestanh, and died for his memory,
And you remember how Peire Vidal ran mad for his
  Wolf Lady

Until she gave him back right reason with one kiss,
And how the Lady of Tripoli came to Jaufre Rudel
As he lay dying, and she too kissed him,
Saying that such a love should not go unrewarded.

Then there is the man in the *langue d'öil* tale
Who fought with no armour but his lady's shift,
And sent it to her all torn and bloody from the battle;
And she kissed it, and put it on over her jewels and silk
As she sat at the high table by the side of her lord,
For she said: 'He did that for me,
And shall I be ashamed of this man's love?'
Clad in the bloody shift she poured wine to the guests,
And all men present praised her for her *grant amor*,
And (says the poet) her lord spake not a word,
For he dared not.

My love is just such a woman
As the supple, high-breasted, high-spirited
Ladies of Provence,
With no fear of the burgesses and the sleek priests
Always strangling life with their unctuous fingers.
She has the gaiety of old Provence,
And I think she would not despise
The unknown lady of Guilhem de Poitiers,
Who was a poet as well as a sovereign prince.
Guilhem had his lady's effigy painted on his long steel shield,
For said he: 'It is fitting I bear her in battle,
Since she so often has borne me in her bed'.

Yet if she is like a lady of old Provence,
Why do I say she is a supple wood-nymph?
But how do you know that those noble women
Whose eyes drew the clerk from the cloister,
The knight's hand from the spear to the lute,

How do you know they were not wood and hill nymphs,
Daughters of the gods, semi-immortals,
Bringing men love and gaiety and beauty,
Fighting in their way, as becomes fair women,
The Jewish gloom and the gloomy Christ?

And again I say she is a wood-nymph
Because she is brave and frank and honest and herself.
Now in this world, which is full of dreary people,
The only fine, vivid characters are those like her
Who are not the epitome of an education, a caste or a class,
But are keen enough and strong enough
To work through prejudices and customs
And to give themselves directly to life and those they love.
Now, if you will think of an English gentleman,
Who is a sort of tidy collection of prejudices;
And if you will think of an American débutante
Waiting in her car to be presented at Court—
You will see the kind of person she is not.
And, unless I am bitterly wrong about her,
Her values are the true values. . . .

And there is yet another reason I call her wood-nymph.
When I was younger they called me a faun
Because I have pointed ears and tell the truth.
And if you know nothing else about wood-nymphs and fauns
You will know the Carnival love song
Lorenzo de' Medici wrote about them. . . .

7

I was walking (you remember)
Slowly up the short drive to (shall I call it 'our'?) house,
Which was pleasantly old and shabby
But bright with new paint.
I took my bag and hat

And followed her into a room
Which I remember so clearly
I could bore you with a long description of it.

The floor was bare wood
With one or two coloured mats she had bought;
The furniture was old, rough French stuff
With a large new unpainted table of plain wood
Holding a huge bowl of spring flowers
And a litter of books and painting things.
There was a good Vlaminck over the hearth
With just those large red smears I like,
And one of those Surréaliste pictures
She thinks she likes
And I try to think I like because she thinks so.
And there were a lot of cheap bright plates and bowls
Such as you buy in French village fairs. . . .
All this I saw in a glance.
But I was still so bemused
I did not drop my bag and take her in my arms,
But stood there like an idiot
Or a good soldier, waiting for orders.
And the next moment it was too late,
For the middle-aged French woman-servant came in
Effusive with *bon soirs* and *madames*.
And my love said: 'Antoinette,
This is Monsieur who has come to stay here—
For a time'.

(And she looked at me sideways with a smile,
Daring me to protest and say 'For always',
But I would not play at being politely gallant with her,
And I had always sworn I would never lie to her.
We had so much to learn about each other,
We had yet to know [though I never doubted it]

Whether we were really made to be lovers to each other,
For you may say—and it is true—
There is far, far more in love than the sexual act,
But if that is wrong all is wrong
And the lovers are not lovers;
Moreover, we cannot know the future
Nor how we shall feel even in a year's time.
It is madness to mortgage the whole future
Even in the delirium of love,
For love is transitory as we are,
And it is dishonest to say 'I shall love you always'
Even if we are convinced of it,
For time passes by, taking all good things,
And there comes a spring morning
And a note from the blackbird in the lilacs
And a glance from bright eyes,
And then what becomes of your 'love you always'?
Only in spans of a few months do we live
And the lover of yesteryear is next year's friend.
So do not say 'I love you for ever',
But say 'I love you now', 'Now I would die for you',
'Now indeed we are one'.
But tomorrow? You cannot answer for tomorrow—
When the apples are red you will find no blackthorn bloom.)

So I did not say 'For always',
As I think she half expected,
For I would not spoil my *vita nuova*
By even a suspicion of humbug.
But Antoinette answered for me, and said: '*Bien, M'dame*',
Which I thought strangely phlegmatic
Considering that this was the miracle of miracles,
And nothing like it had ever happened in the world before—
That two lovers should meet in a small house in France
Alone together between sea and land and sky,

And the heart of at least one of them
Pouring out tenderness and devotion and desire
Like the tall fountain in the Luxembourg
Perpetually pouring and never failing. . . .

And my love said:
'Antoinette will show you your rooms,
You have two rooms there to yourself,
And you are forbidden to come into mine
Except when I invite you.'
So I laughed and went upstairs.
The rooms were just as I would have them,
Large and bare and plenty of bookshelf space,
For somehow I always collect books
As squirrels collect nuts, without thinking about it.
Among the books she had put for me were her own.
I took them down and held them in my hand,
For are they not part of her?

I began to dress in an old flannel suit,
But then I stopped, for I said to myself:
'If she is true woman—and who dare deny it?—
She will want to look beautiful to the man who loves her;
And though she must certainly be most beautiful
With no clothes on at all,
She will have to wear something, because of Antoinette.
And no doubt she will put on the dress
Which she thinks sets her off best,
With just the right amount of red on her lips
And perhaps the right touch of the eye pencil,
And the jewels she would like me to remember
That she wore on our first night alone together.
She will do that partly for herself
(Although there is no other woman to see her,
Which is the main reason for these dress combats)

But chiefly—let me flatter myself—for me,
Because she knows I love her,
And because men like to see women well-dressed,
And also because I am a sort of a poet
And shall notice the details
As well as the general effect.
Now, why shouldn't a man dress for a woman,
Especially when he loves her devoutly?'

So I got out my evening clothes,
Which are pretty old and worn and out-of-date,
But at any rate the intention was there.
I was just getting them out of the bag
When I began to tremble in the legs,
And my head went round, and I had to sit down.
You must remember I had travelled for thirty hours,
Too excited to sleep or eat more than a snatch,
And in the last hour I had lived intensely,
Passing from great pain to great happiness;
And in life we are so unaccustomed to happiness
That it is harder sometimes to bear happiness than pain. . . .

I got my tie straight somehow,
And went downstairs to the room we were to dine in.
Like the others it was plain,
But filled with her presence,
The life of someone who loves intelligence and beauty.
And there was she herself, standing by the table,
Looking up at me with rather a wistful smile—
I suppose she was thinking of past lovers
And how it was all dead and how this too would die.
How the months and the years slip away from us!
How faint grow the memories of the old loves!
But then how sweet, how sweet is the new love!
And if you die when you are still beloved and in love

The gods have done much for you.

But all I thought and saw then was my love
Standing by the table in her bright dress
And her bright eyes and a bright jewel on her breast—
Which was because I had said long ago
I would like to hang the Evening Star on her breast.
There was no more hesitation in me,
But I went to her and took her gently by the hand,
And held her gently to me,
And I put my lips close upon her lips.
Lightly and gently she rested in my arms,
I could feel her warm right breast under my heart.
And her thigh and knee folded against mine,
My right hand held hers and my left embraced her;
I saw her eyes close, and mine closed too,
As I kissed her with the kisses of my mouth. . . .

How long we stood there I do not know;
Time and the world disappeared
And I only knew I held her and kissed her mouth—
My whimsical nymph of the woods,
My high-breasted, high-spirited lady of Provence. . . .
And suddenly Antoinette set down the soup tureen
With a crash, and said: '*V'la M'dme*', quite calmly.
And though you could not call lovers of our age children,
We started asunder and blushed like very young lovers.
But as Antoinette went out, I kissed my love's hand,
And those two kisses meant that all was right between us
After the long days and nights of pain and absence,
And meant that we should be happy together.

8

Now, I don't quite know whether I should linger
Or hurry over this.

If I pleased myself I should linger
Because it makes me so happy to re-dream this dream,
Which, like life itself, is the vision of a vision.
But then, when I think it might seem tiresome to her,
I am tempted to hurry. . . .

9

I think we were both very happy at dinner,
For after we had made the compact of that kiss
And knew that we were each other's—
As much as man and woman can be,
'For a time', as she had said to Antoinette—
It was very easy to talk gaily and easily.
I said a number of good things which surprised me,
And I'm quite sure they surprised her,
Because I had always been very silent in her presence before,
For if one cannot speak out what is in one's heart
And cannot show what one is really feeling,
It is impossible—at least for me—to talk freely.

I was still too excited to eat much,
And, of course, I wasted so much time looking at her
When I thought she wouldn't notice it,
That I was always miles behind with my course,
And was scolded for making her look like a glutton.
I thought Antoinette's soup marvellous,
And then there was some fish bought from the boat that day,
And one of those inspired ragouts
Which you can only find in France,
And some fruit.
I fear I left more on my plate than I ate,
For how can one eat with one's heart still thumping
With the first kiss from a wood-nymph?
But my love made me taste the red wine
Which she had bought from Père Somebody on the hill,

And then the white wine from a little *auberge*
At a quaint village, oh miles away,
So I tasted them both, and praised them,
For they were really good pure wine
Such as you can never get in England
And hardly even in Paris.
And then after the dessert, although I protested
I was already so drunk with love
That it was quite unsafe to give me anything else,
She insisted I should taste the amazing new liqueur
She had discovered in Spain last year.
Before she could get the cigars, I brought out my case
And handed it to her; and she saw
That I had filled it with the kind she likes best.
So she took one, because she knew it would please me,
And that I had been thinking of her when I bought them;
And I took one of hers.
As I went over to hold the match for her,
I could not help bending down to kiss her hair
Which was smooth and glossy in the soft light
Like those crisp ilex leaves on the Pincian.
We went on talking quietly and happily as we smoked,
In the quiet room of that quiet house,
And were very happy, with no fever of impatience
Like young and inexperienced lovers
Always in too much of a hurry to join together
And generally punished by disappointment.
It was not as if we had any mystery to learn
(Except that it is always a mystery why two people love)
And we knew we should not be like the Romantic poet
Who found that 'even the bed of love
Which in the imagination had seemed the giver of all good
Was no more than a wine-cup in the drinking and as soon
    finished'—
Which shows what sort of a clumsy ass he was—

And so, like wise people the world over,
We enjoyed the present to the full.

A little later I said:
'It is so much warmer here than in England,
Couldn't we go down to the sea for a moment?'
So she fetched a cloak and we went out.
She showed me the garden in the dim moonlight—
There was a half-moon among the dimmer stars
And a good deal of light cloud—
And as I had scarcely seen it by daylight
It all looked strange and mysterious and beautiful.
We took a little path down to the shore,
And she said:
'There is the place where we can bathe tomorrow,
And there is a little boat we can row about in
Or go fishing, if you like.'
Softly the garden leaves rustled in the evening wind,
Softly the veiled moonlight breathed on her face,
Softly the light sea fell on the rock and sand
With low continuous sound like the murmur of two lovers.

I found a small garden bench,
Half-surrounded by shrubs and facing the sea.
I sat down on it and took her on my knees.
And this time I held her very close to me
So that through our thin clothes our bodies were espoused.
Oh, I made no intimate caresses,
For a long time I did not even kiss her,
But sat with her body pressed to mine in the darkness
Mysteriously communing with her,
The mysterious essence of me with her mysterious essence;
A chance meeting of twin atoms in a dark infinity,
Oh, so brief a meeting in the infinite ages;
And what words cannot say and even kisses only hint at

We said to each other by silence through our veiled bodies.
And still like an inexhaustible fountain
There came from me that continuous outpouring
Of devotion and tenderness and desire.
Through so many centuries of longing
I had thought of such communion with her
In the night, in the silence, we two alone, together.
After all the pain and the heart-break,
To slide into this delicious peace
And to be at one with my lady of Provence
Whom I adored so, was too much happiness.
My muscles began to tremble again and my head was dizzy;
And she said: 'What is it, are you unhappy?'
'No, it is too much happiness, after much pain——'
And she said: 'You are tired out with your journey,
And over-wrought. You must go to bed'.
But I said: 'No! No! I wish this evening might never end;
Shall I ever be so happy again?'
And I began to kiss her mouth
Until we both were dazed and trembling. . . .

10

Why is it that my words begin to flag
When hitherto they have flowed so rapidly
That I could not even stop to choose among them?
But you have guessed it—
I am drawing towards the end of my dream,
And my words falter because never again,
No, never again shall I re-live my dream
And all its happiness and emotions and sensations.
For it is all hopeless—she does not love me,
And there is the world and what it says.
I have deceived myself—she does not love me,
And all I have written with so much faith and ardour
Never happened and never will happen.

If I showed such delusions about ordinary life
They would shut me up in a mad-house,
For I have lost the sense of the thin boundary
Between what is and is not,
Between the real and the ideal,
The true and the imaginary.
She does not love me.

Suppose you were a rather clumsy glass-maker
And one day a miracle happened,
From your breath grew a miraculous slender glass bowl
More exquisite than any Venetian glass.
And just as you were marvelling at its beauty
And thinking how your whole life would be changed,
Some invisible hand poured in the traditional poison
So that in a flash the miraculous cup collapsed
And crumbled to a little dust in your hand . . .
'She does not love me' is the poison.—

11

'Good night', she said, as we stood by her bedroom door,
'Good night, sleep well and dream of me,
Antoinette will call you tomorrow morning,
And you can bathe in the sea with me or not, as you like.'
And I thought:
'She said I was never to enter her room uninvited.
Perhaps she does not want to lie with me tonight,
Perhaps she does not want to lie with me at all;
Or perhaps—which is more flattering—
Since she knows how important it is
That this should be right and perfect,
She thinks I am too tired from my long journey
And from all the emotions of tonight,
And that it is better to wait. She may be right.'
So I bent and kissed her hand devoutly, saying:

'Good night, good night, my love, good night'.

But as I slowly undressed, I was thinking hard.
For once my *esprit* is on the *escalier*
It moves with admirable rapidity. And I thought:
'This is all nonsense. I am tired, but not so tired.
Am I a boy to be awkward and ineffectual?
(Hamlet should have said: "Brief as a boy's embrace.")
I'm such a slow-witted fool
I didn't even ask if I might lie with her,
And of course, she gave me the chance not to.
True, she did not invite me,
But she did not say I was not to come'.

At that moment, as I stood quite naked, thinking,
I saw myself in a long mirror,
And was surprised to see I was almost handsome
And how bright and clear my eyes looked.
And I said to myself:
'By God, if I do not love her tonight it is treason,
Treason to Love, to her, to myself, to the miracle
Which has drifted together for a fraction of eternity
Us two frail atoms with our lives and passions.
I might die in the night, there might be an earthquake,
England may have declared war today,
Tomorrow she may not love me . . .'

I wrapped myself in a thin gown
And in a second was tapping at her door,
Not timidly and not too loudly,
But as one who says: 'I mean to come in',
And I heard her clear voice say: 'Come in !'

She was sitting up in bed, reading,
Dressed in a thin green silk chemise

Cut so low that one could nearly see her breast-points,
And a little green coat over it wide open in front;
And she said: 'Is there anything the matter?
Has Antoinette forgotten something?'
I made no answer, but kneeled on one knee beside her,
Put both my hands on her breasts
And looked deep, deep into her eyes.
Slowly she put her arms about me
And slowly she pressed her body against mine. . . .

12

I shall say no more,
Nothing of how we were lovers,
How I was her lover and she my woman.
Though once I meant to tell her—the real her—
How in the dream she was so beautiful
And so ardent a woman lover,
And all we did and all we said.
But I cannot tell it even to her,
For the mysteries that are spoken by two bodies,
The bodies of two lovers, so ardent, so beautiful,
Cannot be said in words, even a lover's words,
Even when the lover is a sort of a poet.

13

Now, although it was long before we slept—
For she allowed me to remain with her,
And I had fallen asleep holding her in my arms
Very gently and tenderly, as a lover does,
While my heart poured out tenderness for her
Like a fountain, like the white Luxembourg fountain,
And I had fallen asleep though I tried to keep awake
To feel my wood-nymph caught so tenderly in my arms
And to listen to her soft low breathing,
And to taste my happiness, because at last

After all the pain and the long empty days
She was there by my side, sleeping, my wild love—
And although I was supposed to be so tired,
Yet I was the first to wake.
I bent over and looked at her as she still slept,
Watching her, the lips a little parted,
The deep eyes hidden with the lashes,
A wisp of hair on her cheek;
And I thought my breath would fail,
My heart stop beating,
So much did·I love her. . . .

She turned her head with slowly-opening eyes and smiled
    at me,
And in a moment she was in my arms,
My mouth on her warm, sleep-warm lips.

It was very late when my love rang,
But Antoinette came in most composedly
Bringing our coffee and her letters.
I huddled down in the clothes
For I was a little abashed
That even a middle-aged French woman-servant
Should see me lying beside my love.
But she said;
'*Monsieur est très pudique, vous voyez*'.
And Antoinette said stolidly: '*Oui, M'dame*'.
And then most unexpectedly,
Leaving us both greatly surprised,
Antoinette smiled most approvingly at us,
And said: '*Soyez bénis, mes enfants,
Soyez heureux, vous êtes encore jeunes*',
And then rushed from the room. . . .

Faint, faint are the voices that come to me,

Fainter and fainter the colours, fainter my dream;
It is passing like the setting rays from still water,
Drifting away like the willow leaves on a cold morning
When they patter so dismally on the frosty ground,
Fading as the colours fade from the roses at twilight,
Growing dim like the eyes of a wounded soldier,
Leaving me, inexorably leaving me. . . .

Yet something I remember. . . .
I remember how my love rose from our bed
And stood naked and unconcerned before me—
For was I not her lover and is she not beautiful?—
While I watched her with the sunlight on her breasts,
As she stood so straight and white by the open window
Saying: 'Today we will not try to work,
But both take a holiday.
Let us have a picnic somewhere and bathe
And take a long drive afterwards. . . .'
My dream is almost broken. . . .

But I remember, dimly I remember
Many more days of sunlight and rain,
Days of hard work and merry playing,
Nights when she read to me in her clear voice
Either from the book she was writing
Or from Elizabethan poets—
Can I ever forget her clear voice reading
'Follow thy saint, follow with accents sweet'?—
And friends came to see us, but did not part us
Although all the world hates lovers.
For a moment the colours of the dream flash brighter. . . .
I remember how I loved her and she loved me,
I remember how so many nights she lay in my arms
In that mysterious communion of love. . . .

At that moment the tall white fountain jet
Fell from its height, crumbled like dust of water;
Like dust of water it fell to a faint bubbling.
Light faded from the Luxembourg
As a heavy cloud from the north engulfed the sun,
And a chill breeze ran over me.
The dream was broken, fallen into dust
Like the white fountain, like a Venetian glass
When the poison is poured in it.
I saw the horror and dreariness of the world
Which they tell me is the real world—the world of dust.
The leaves were not coloured like the leaves
I had seen in our garden, and were all dusty,
And the drab French people passing
Had dust on their shoes and clothes.
You could see the dust driving as the wind rose
And hurried it whirling over the pool to the fountain,
And it seemed to choke me as I walked blindly away.

Then I knew the bitterness and the drabness of the real,
And all the bitterness I have tried to quell
Went whirling over me like a wild sea,
And I thought of all the old unhappy things
Which I had quite forgotten in my dream.

For a moment I stood by Bailly's statue
Opposite the façade of the palace,
Remembering the Revolution.
And I thought how Mirabeau once made a great speech,
And the whole Convention rose and shouted to him,
And while they were still cheering wildly
A man leaned over to him and said: '*Sophie est morte*'.
And Mirabeau turned ice-pale and left abruptly

Though they were still cheering him. . . .

And I said to myself: 'She does not love me,
It was only a dream, a fool's dream, a fool's paradise'.
Crumbled into dust my dream like the dying fountain
Which collapsed in a dust of white water,
Dust like the crumbled Venetian glass,
Dusty like the dusty wind-whirls about me,
A world of grey-white dust.

I stooped to the ground,
And with my finger-tip
Took a tiny pinch of dust
And put it to my lips—

It had a very bitter taste.

THE EATEN HEART

THE EATEN HEART

1

UNDER the reign of Mr Bloom
When the loud machines beat on our minds,
We, that are children of despair,
Who see or think we see so clearly
Through Philoctetes' pain and Timon's rage
How all hope's vain, all effort null;
We that tremble between two worlds,
Half-regretting the old dead Europe
Crumbling and melancholy as a deserted palace
When the last king of the line has long been dead,
Frightened yet moulded by the cold hard patterns
Beaten upon life by the loud machines—
What do we know of love?

A man or woman might die for love
And be glad in dying;
But who would die for sex?
Die for food or drink?

Better turn monk
And keep your sperm for God
And hard despair.
Will you die for a blind hot instinct,
The rut of insect and beast,
(*O stab the words home till the wound is deep*
To dull a fiercer pain)
Die for a female mammal—
Two breasts and a curled slit?
(*O stab, till you sob with pain.*)

Yet women have loved, and men have died for them.

2

O Love—Euripides speaks—
O love through the eyes you speed desire,
In our souls you breathe delight.
Come not to me, O Love, with an escort of woe,
Harry me not beyond the strength of a man.

3

Women have loved and men have died for them,
And a woman has died for the man she loved.
Die? What! Die for remembered pleasures
Or pleasures hoped for or pleasures dreamed of,
Smooth caresses, the shock of spasms?

But I say there is more in all this
Than the delicate friction of two skins. . . .

Do you know you live in a prison?
Do you know your own loneliness?
For long years you are unaware of it,
Move and act in the world,
Talk, laugh, eat, play, make love,
Believe yourself alive,
And never know you are in deathly solitude.

All through the years you move among men and women,
And you are imprisoned away from them, and they from you.
But within you is a world, a small human world,
A mysterious unconscious or half-conscious you,
Dumbly yearning in a wordless apathy
To break from the prison in a rush of ecstasy,
In a tumultuous outpouring of itself,
A divine frenzy of tenderness and devotion,
To meet its sister world.

Sun after sun rolls from dawn to setting,
Inhuman constellations wheel above you,
A generation of buds points the bare spring branches,
A generation of dying leaves drifts past you;
They who were children when you played a man's part
Smile at your memories, never knew your dead,
And lonely, lonely is the spirit within you,
Lonelier than any Bastille prisoner,
Lonelier than a barren Aegean islet.

And yet you do not know it,
Feel only a vague mysterious yearning,
A dim malaise, a something wanting,
Whether your days are mirthful or bleak with despair—
The cold despair of the mind,
Not the worse despair of the soul.
And suddenly, unawares, there is a meeting of eyes. . . .

4

It is true of course, as Euripides says,
That what enters by the eyes is desire,
But desire for what?

Desire, indeed, desire for the meeting of bodies—
For our bodies are we, and the 'soul' is a metaphor
To express the unknown in ourselves,
As 'God' is the unknown in the universe;
And primordial urgent desire
That life should be continued.

This is the love of savages,
For, though the savage will kill for desire,
He will not die for it;
Where men are primitive, desire must be primitive,
And therefore women are slaves and chattels

As in some respects they still are—
And it is right they should be,
For they lack the magnanimity of free men.

With our hands and breasts we speak mysterious things
Which the filter of speech rejects,
And only through the known, exterior body
Do we reach the mysterious unknown within.

The desire I strive to express,
The desire I believe Euripides means,
(For a woman like Phaedra does not die
Because a man refuses her bed)
This desire is a complex thing
Both civilised and primitive.
(For civilisation is not only a complexity of material needs,
But a complexity of passionate and mental needs,
The discovery and enjoyment of ourselves
As well as of what is outside ourselves.)

When desire speeds through the eyes
For a moment there is strange tumult
In the whole nature of man or woman,
And in a flash all life is changed.
For all the known and the unknown in them
Are acutely alert and clamouring
In a tumult of pain and joy
Such as I think Philoctetes felt
When he grasped the hand of Neoptolemus,
A friend, and the son of a friend, a saviour,
The breaker of bonds,
Releaser from a ten years prison.

(I have a right to re-interpret a Greek tragedy:
Take it as an expression of human loneliness,

The dreadful inevitable loneliness of the human soul,
The tragedy of delusive joy
At the hope of recognition and release,
The tragedy of real pain and bitterness
When the hope vanishes before human treachery
And human incomprehension and indifference,
The tragedy which only a god could undo
If there were a god—
O Sophoclean irony, your hard serenity!)

There in Philoctetes the tragedy is stated,
Dramatised, sublimated in a pure serenity
Strangely brooding aloof over human loneliness.

And what is true of the tortured Philoctetes—
Who has nothing left but pride and despair—
Is universal, true today, true of ourselves.

With us the tragedy is more complex and incoherent;
It is softer and perhaps a little mawkish
Because it is so complicated with sexual desire
Which leaves us so exposed to ridicule,
And we fear ridicule more than we fear the gods.

I, brooding alone over lonely miseries about me,
Think that for many, for most, perhaps,
This tragedy never happens,
The moment never arrives,
The miracle never occurs,
The need is never felt.
(They may be unhappy in other ways,
But in this profound way they are not unhappy.)

But to others the moment comes
And the whole nature is set free,

Is conscious of its totality, affirms itself,
Escapes from negative existence, and lives.
This is what happens to men and women
When we see they are suddenly changed
And are surprised at the change.

But—brief was the joy of Philoctetes—
All that passionate outpouring of self,
That sudden release, that immense deliverance,
Recoil on themselves in blind despair and apathy
If the response is null or inadequate,
If the sister-world is not really a sister-world.

Most lives are monologues, and so grow poorer;
But conceive the riches if the response is there,
Question and answer, change and interchange,
Positive life.

If the response is there, a life is fulfilled,
For the dialogue life of those two natures
Grows richer a thousand-fold
Than the two monologue lives lived separately,
Dwindling in their own loneliness.

If there is some response, a reaching-out,
Either to the full extent of a lesser world
Or the partial extent of an equal or greater world,
There remains a poignant memory, a dream—
Laura or Beatrice.

I do not deny the body, I praise it—
That is where Petrarch and Dante err—
But the tragedy of thwarted sexual desire is nothing,
The true tragedy is that of inner loneliness,
Philoctetes agonising on his lonely isle . . .

5

Now, under the reign of Mr Bloom,
When the strange machines have killed the old Europe
Which seems so easy and pleasant to us
Because it was ungeometric, and is dead,
I brood on the strange unhappy lives
And the hard unhappy faces, sometimes so beautiful
But strangely hard.

We were right, yes, we were right
To smash the false idealities of the last age,
The humbug, the soft cruelty, the mawkishness,
The heavy tyrannical sentimentality,
The inability to face facts, especially new facts;
All of which linger on so damnably among us.

We were right to question and to destroy,
Pitching out gods and fools, lumber and riches,
Clearing away the falsities and pretensions.
We are right too when we turn,
Even if with infinite regret, from the old dead Europe,
And face the hard new world, the world of machines;
For we cannot kill the machines,
And if we fight them, they will kill us.

I think we were right to go groping in all forbidden places,
Uncovering horrors politely forgotten
And facing them too,
Making ourselves hard for the hard age of machines.
I like the men and women of my age,
I like their hardness,
For though we are a battered and rather bitter set,
Still we have faced the facts, we have been pretty honest.
But, sitting here brooding over the hard faces,

I wonder if we have not rejected too much,
If we have not hardened ourselves too much
Making it impossible to break out of our self-prisons,
As if Philoctetes had exiled himself?

Of course, you can say it is the War,
But you cannot put everything down to the War
Nor to the machines either.
We have mistaken the problem, overlooked the tragedy.
We are all rather like Philoctetes,
But we do not know it.
It is not true to say that life is more difficult—
Materially it is easier,
Only for the spirit is it more difficult
Because, like the heroes of Sophocles,
We have looked too closely
Or too deeply into realities
And know, or think we know, that nothing is worth achieving.
But, gazing back at the old dead Europe,
I think perhaps there is one thing worth achieving—
Escape the fate of Philoctetes, the essential solitude,
Achieve release, so that one's total nature
At all points meets another's
Whereby life becomes positive and immeasurably enriched.
Then something that is not oneself, a person,
Becomes so precious one would gladly die for it
And would certainly, or almost certainly,
Die or kill oneself if suddenly deprived of it . . .

6

Then I remembered the old Provence tale of the Eaten Heart,
Which, like the tale of Philoctetes, is a sort of myth,
But filled with profound meaning if you can see it.

For it has the savage desire which can only grasp or kill
And the other love which is the complete exchange of two
    natures,
And in the dreadful symbol of the eaten heart
It shows perhaps how a woman devours a man's life,
But it also shows how the man's gift of himself is total,
And the manner of her death shows how her response is total.

Here you have the last variety of this tragedy;
For if we assume that the lovers really were released,
That the gift and the response were total,
Then we see how a woman's vanity and a man's imprudence
And the brutality of the world of men
(Who always envy the happiness of others
And hate nothing so much as the perfect communing of
    lovers)
How these things bring a sudden and tragic ending
Leaving no fate for both but death.

We have lost or thrown away
The power to live in this positive tragic intensity—
For if life is not a tragedy it is nothing.

And even if the release takes place
And the dialogue of the two natures is perfect,
Still, the end must be tragic. It is easy to see that.
Though the fundamental, essential tragedy perhaps
(Some say 'of course')
Is not death, but birth.
But if Euripides means what I think he means,
His prayer is vain;
None of those chosen can escape the escort of woe
And the harrying beyond the strength of a man.

7

Not in a vortex of confusion
Not in a low sucking marsh
Of stagnant habit
O gods let us die

Not under roofs of acquiescence
Guide us O moon
Bright face averted though loved
Not under those

Hot hounds of disaster
Swift steel of despair
Launch at us freely
Grant us clean shrift O gods
Pity us never

8

But was it this I meant to say?
No, for what we mean to say is never said.
It was a weak squabble with despair,
A verbose quibbling about Helen's hair.
What was he saying? That we talk too much?
By God, we do, and seldom utter truth.

Lucretius sat in his columned porch
On a Roman deck-chair, looking out to sea,
Watching men drown with eager
Scientific curiosity.
Watch me drown and afterwards
Tell me if I did it gracefully.
Ah, that's the thing, just do it gracefully
And listen to the grateful loud applause.
But, above all things, let it not discompose you,
Let not your earnestness appear . . .

'Helen, you ate my heart.'

'No, no, what a muddle you're in.
It was not Helen, but Margarida.'

'Well, but has she played her part?
She ought to fall from the lip of the tower,
And there she is prettily eating fruit,
Or are we both buried in Perpignan,
In a single tomb in the southern aisle
Which gave much scope to the sculptor's skill
And made him his name,
With an epitaph penned by the King himself?

'Then this is one of those mortal dreams
Which come to dead men under the paving,
When the last cowled friar has shuffled to bed
And the church itself lies dead with the dead?'

Hush, you dead man, hush, be at rest;
The lettered slab is firm above you,
Solid the effigy, fixed the shield.
Your sighs and struggles will never move them,
Time will wreck them, but not you—
Hush, you dead man, act a dead man's part
And leave to the living the life you lost.
You shall have prayers and masses,
All things we choose to give the dead,
But the thing you ask for you shall not have.

9
Pray for the soul of Guilhem de Cabestanh,
Pray for the knight of the Eaten Heart.

SHORT POEMS

1

TROY's down
and an old woman nods in the sun,
Electra:

'She with her eyes, and hair
red as the blood on her slender hands,
and swift eddy of passions,
dust in the rock-tomb under the gold garments.

Kings shed blood for her sake—
and I, the virtuous, the serf's bride,
an old woman trembling in chilly sunlight,
a king's daughter,
but not the lover or mother of kings.

Great deeds were wrought by the King, my father,
but the passion in a woman's blood
swept him moaning to the grave.
No man has shed blood for my sake.

I armed my brother's hand
but shrank and trembled and wept
when the sword pierced her womb,
the woman men loved.

It was I who killed her;
who but a woman could have hated her so much?
Cold, cold, and an end to her hot loves.

But who has loved me,
what man shed blood for my sake?'

Troy's down,
long down,
and an old woman trembles in the sun.

2

Tender as early leaves on fragile boughs,
Slender as Isis,
Taut as supple metal—
How shall you be praised?

Syrinx no Pan shall pluck
For waxen reed-pipes;
You yourself music
Entranced and entrancing,
Piercing men's loins and breasts—
Pied-Piper of lovers.

Frail mountain-ash
Weighted with coral fruit-clusters,
Your branches hold me,
Leaves murmur touching me.
My hand rests lightly upon you.

II

You are flowers and gems,
Flower-star-eyes!
What shall we gather to please you?
Corals and jade and lapis.
Steal the lapis from the Gesú
To make you necklaces and charms,
Jade from the Antipodes
Negro chains and beads
Blue Mexican pebbles.
But no, no pearls
The stones of dowagers and virgins.

Ah! but your flower-like
More precious even than your gem-like,
Your tenderness—
Here is cyclamen
That stands so stiff and pink
And has such honey at its heart,
And wild narcissus
Soft and scented like your little breasts,
And one carnation like an open jewel.

3

Gold head by black head
laid close on the pillow,
ripe yellow muscat grapes
warm from low sunlit slopes
mingled with the dark shy clusters
of cool black grapes
from the shy dark mountain side.

Gold, sun-scented clusters,
black, violet-bloomed clusters,
exquisite fruition
of the mysterious vine
rooted in the dark red flesh of men,
in the aching ardent bodies of men—
what wine, what wine shall be poured from you
when you are crushed
(for you must be crushed,
the exquisite grape clusters
golden and black must be crushed,
give up their perfume and their strength)
when you are crushed in the hot wine-press?

For the ripe grape
with its exquisite mysterious wine,

its taste of perfumed life,
dreads not the hot encompassing press,
but yearns to be pressed into smooth wine
to stir the dark red flesh of men
where the vine roots
that bears the grape clusters
black clusters and gold clusters.

And the dark clusters
droop tenderly over the gold grapes,
and tender leaves of the vine
and faint delicate tendrils
drift together in a soft murmuring wind,
rippling over them,
blowing them together and apart.
Crush black grape and gold,
for our lips parch for the wine,
the wine of fulfilment,
the wine of reconciling,
the wine of peace.
For to drink that ardent mysterious wine
(ardent and mysterious as the bodies of men)
is a thing ultimate and positive,
a release of the body and the spirit.
If you attain that fulfilment,
achieve that reconciling,
then you achieve an ultimate peace,
Dionysiac peace
among the gold and black grape clusters
so mysteriously reborn
with all their fine bloom and potency
after they are crushed in the hot wine-press.
White fingers of Maenads
in the frenzy of the god
tear apart,

rend morsel from morsel
the dark red flesh of men,
the phallos-bearers,
the indispensable servitors
of the god's sacrifice,
impetuously and in frenzy
tear out quivering life.

But the crushed grapes bloom again,
and the torn body lives again
in fulfilment
and reconciling
and peace.

This is the mystic sacrifice
of the Dionysiac tearing of the flesh
and crushing of the grape-clusters.
The old gods are the most living,
the primitive mysteries the most purifying,
the most ancient symbols the truest.

Black grape and gold grape
and dark flesh rent.

4

Be not too eager
impetuously to intervene,
for these are subtle growths
hard to control.

How easily the spring may swerve
to an empty wind.
Cold irony, to grasp so soon
the fleshless hand.

This was a delicate thing

lies broken here,
as if a shaft of light
should kill the dawn.

There can be no appeal
from waste and death,
nothing for us to act
or hope or speak.

All speech, all movement vain,
all hope defeat;
useless to say farewell,
useless to weep.

Drink, since you must, this strange
foretaste of death,
and suffer that despair
to share your bed.

5

Be unto me as sunlight
Revealed and revealing the
Infinite life-spaces, hitherto darkly
Guarded by death-dragons; and
In beautiful radiance
Touch me alive with slender rays.

II

Lips that never lost their sweetness,
Nor formed a bitter line;
Delicate frail face and forehead,
Eyes of pain,
Eyes of a sweet hurt child,
Eyes that touch me to the heart—
O that for long and long

I might feel your presence,
Eyes with a dawn in them.

III

When I returned to London
After a long absence,
The beautiful scarlet motor-buses
Seemed like gay lacquered coaches.
A little later they appeared
As sinister red hearses
Conveying the dead souls
Of a nation.

IV

Think well of me, but not too well.
I would not seem to fail you,
As I must,
If you esteem me overmuch;
But love me more than well,
For too much love
Was never known beneath the sun,
And only your great love
Can soothe that shame
Of knowing me unworthy of your love.

V

Yes, I have cried my pain aloud
But left the deeper bitterer grief unspoken;
Yes, I have been misjudged
But thought it proper to respect my judges;
Yes, I have been betrayed
But paid the traitors with ironic kisses;
Yes, I have suffered wrongs,
Been punished for my virtues,
Found my best gifts counted as my worst sins. . . .

But what of that?
You see I smile and smile, and am a villain.

6

and I shall wait
while the huge wind
passes
whitening the barren blue sea-acres
and the wild olive-trees
while the wind sobs
and violently knocks at window and door
shaking the room with a passion of grief
until my heart shakes with it
I shall wait
in the still places of the soul
behind the talk and tears
I shall wait
and behind other sighs and kisses
and less urgent thoughts
I shall wait
because I have looked into eyes
of dawn and twilight
kissed the lips of her
who is my sister and my flesh
and the blood shaking in my heart
I shall wait
yes I shall wait
for a word the beckoning of a white hand
I shall wait yes yes
and the inevitable heart-break
I shall await

7

They say the lion and
but here lizards life-flashes

over stormy rocks why
do the english hate life
but so does raucous italy
fingering cento lire
                              but
that oleander mouth is
diverse spirit wavering
                              in agate eyes
the inner fire consumes
                              and life renews

8

Unyielding
there is no way out
mosaic mask threatens and laughs
that blood was wasted
so were his hers mine
I always knew that brought the **gravest pang**
there is no way out
who said so? he said so
no I said so
up those winding stairs
so long and tedious to mount alone
always the mosaic mask
that nothing says and says too much
there is no way out
except the inevitable final plunge
and that's not soon
and yet too soon
round and up they wind
and up and round
blind feeling with finger tips
up and round
there is no way out
but why have entered?

yes why have entered?
entered? well the mask said enter
so beautiful a mask
I forgot the blood
so beautifully so like a god
said enter I forgot the blood
ran stumbling upwards too eagerly
then the mask changed
and yes there is no way out

9

not to define nor plan too far nor
grasp too eagerly with the child's
so absolute stomachic yearning
to absorb but continuity
means something and love grows
river-like tree-like yes
but not for ever digging at the roots
how grows it nor with plummet
anxious brow my river does it
flow as rippling-sweet and
flows it wider deeper as it should
strive not to over-strive the
sudden flutter of song lives
on girl's lips men's hearts ah
let the river flow tree leaf
                        and most
shun the death-instinct love
is love because of death
love's opposite but confound
them never that way lies
hell annihilation
                but
                    you

to you o poet

for as I sit here
nervous restless
unable to think
in the intolerable anguish of waiting
waiting
for the swift tap at the door
the small blue telegram
I shall open with trembling hands
waiting
while time nods a haggard look at hell
and the dice of passion are thrown
with my life the gage
and still she has not answered
now in the drifting agony of minutes
your words are beautiful to me,
and the passion alive in them
answers the wordless passion in my blood
and they you praise seem she
for whom I wait

11

we'll have no stories of dead women
to allay our loves

grey smoke drifts through the grey-green olives
voices of children playing
broken rhythms of people passing
soft roll of the noon-blue sea
now
now
and the turn of your head
a new softening of old pride

IN MEMORY OF WILFRED OWEN

I HAD half-forgotten among the soft blue waters
And the gay-fruited arbutus of the hill
Where never the nightingales are silent,
And the sunny hours are warm with honey and dew;

I had half-forgotten as the stars slid westward
Year after year in grave majestic order,
In the strivings and in the triumphs of manhood,
The world's voice, and the touch of beloved hands.

But I have never quite forgotten, never forgotten
All you who lie there so lonely, and never stir
When the hired buglers call unheeded to you,
Whom the sun shall never warm nor the frost chill.

Do you remember . . . but why should you remember?
Have you not given all you had, to forget?
Oh, blessed, blessed be Death! They can no more vex you,
You for whom memory and forgetfulness are one.

1931

EPILOGUE TO 'DEATH OF A HERO'

ELEVEN years after the fall of Troy,
We, the old men—some of us nearly forty—
Met and talked on the sunny rampart
Over our wine, while the lizards scuttled
In dusty grass, and the crickets chirred.

Some bared their wounds;
Some spoke of the thirst, dry in the throat,
And the heart-beat, in the din of battle;
Some spoke of intolerable sufferings,
The brightness gone from their eyes
And the grey already thick in their hair.

And I sat a little apart
From the garrulous talk and old memories,
And I heard a boy of twenty
Say petulantly to a girl, seizing her arm:
'Oh, come away, why do you stand there
Listening open-mouthed to the talk of old men?
Haven't you heard enough of Troy and Achilles?
Why should they bore us for ever
With an old quarrel and the names of dead men
We never knew, and dull forgotten battles?'

And he drew her away,
And she looked back and laughed
As he spoke more contempt of us,
Being now out of hearing.

And I thought of the graves by desolate Troy
And the beauty of many young men now dust,
And the long agony, and how useless it all was.
And the talk still clashed about me

Like the meeting of blade and blade.

And as they two moved further away
He put an arm about her, and kissed her;
And afterwards I heard their gay distant laughter.

And I looked at the hollow cheeks
And the weary eyes and the grey-streaked heads
Of the old men—nearly forty—about me;
And I too walked away
In an agony of helpless grief and pity.

LIFE QUEST

LIFE QUEST

1

RAIN in the Pyrenees . . .

Tonight they will dance till dawn at Biarritz
And the *milors* will see their fun is clean
Dancing among the gold-topped bottles
Euro-African and clean
Between the futile mountains and the silly sea.

These are the Koh-i-noor
The diamond point of living light
Cresting the shadowy pyramid of the dead.

Hail to Thee, Amon-Ra,
And Oom to Thee, O Bouddha.

Tonight it will be very lonely
In the woods of Roncesvalles,
There will be a sighing in the damp branches
A cold smell from the leafy ground
In the blackness of pilgrim shadows.

Listen, listen until hearing dies
For the echoes of the ivory horn,
Stare your eyes to stone
But you will not see . . .

. . . the living among the dead.

The life quest falters
And the ankh unlocks no door.

Shall we seek along the dock yards
Over the muddy asphalt paper-strewn?
Shall we follow the trams to the well at
   the world's end?

Ponce de Leon—he drank of many a
   spring
In virgin islands burned with tropic
   gold
And rusty armour grates his ribs.

I have seen the concrete pylons
Ranked in the Lombard plains
Raising stiff arms to the Duce or the
   sky,
But what they meant I could not tell.

I have seen the planes go up and down
And none brought tidings from the
   Golden Isles
But there's many a crooked stone in
   Northern France.

3

At Irun in the night I heard
Harsh voices from the hostile street
Where the mirrored balconies were blank and
dark.
'*Adios*' they said '*adios*',
But they could not part,
Afraid of the darkness
That was dark as death.

'*Adios*'—but once more, only once more
Let me hear my friend's voice, once more
Let me see his shape in the blackness,
'*Adios*'—but let me touch him once more,
Oh, let me know we are not dead in the dead
night.

'*Adios*.'

4

O eloquent just and mighty death.
In the morning I walked in Santillana
Under a sky crystal and cobalt
Shot with the arrow heads of swifts,
Santillana half-dead city of flies,
Reeking of cow dung splashed on broken cobbles,
Half-dead city—O florid heraldries
Stonily boasting the pride of dead hidalgos.

Santillana!
Your lordly balconies are red
With the common flowers of your servants' sons.

Dead the hidalgós, dead the canons,

Dead the learning, wrecked the royal gifts;
None to walk the streets and the cloister
With sword or prayer for the glory of God and
    Spain.

Santillana! Santillana!

Who mourns for Santillana?
Who guards these honoured bones?

O noble lords, your tombs are broken,
Horrors of filth and common rubbish
Mix with your princely dust.

5

Grimaldi bones smeared with red ochre
That apes bright blood the life-giver
Conjured in vain as age by age
Rubble and drift and ashes built a tomb
A stiff and rocky shroud
                            but saved no soul.

More splendid fantasy robed Osiris dead
In gold and natron under pyramids,
Furnished the palace-grave for an eternity
The Ka has never entered.

O Isis, Mother Isis, was it worth the quest?

6

In the beginning
But we do not know the beginning,
In the end
But we do not know the end.

The sun was not and that was yesterday,
Tomorrow he dies and what is changed?

The stage of this little world's too narrow,
The amphitheatre of the stars too wide.

Life's a poor tragedy whose end's foretold.

7

We shall not see, we shall never see
Gold islands of the blest in sweeter air
Where all are young and happy and there is
    peace.

The Ship of the Dead has never come to port,
It never started.

We have dreamed
These sixty centuries we have dreamed
Our hopes and fears into shapes of many gods.

The earth is haggard with our ruined shrines,
With crumbling temples, dusty tombs,
Dead bibles teaching the way of life
And many a saviour who never saved . . .

The resurrection and the life.

Shall we make new gods
Of the sine and tensor
And skate the outside edge
Of the finite world?

Let's have a picnic
With Aknaton and Jeans
In the centre of the sun
Filling our waistcoat pockets
With nuclei by the ton.

Let's hitch our waggon to a spiral nebula
And live for ever backwards
Faster than light—
Oh to unsmoke that mathematical cigar!

Let's seek salvation in magnetic fields—
Skoal to the deathless proton!

Let's build a New Church
In shape like unto a lucky horseshoe,
And magnify the Lord, the Sacred Magnet,
With clouds of chlorine incense
And reverent muttering of surds.

Let's build a tabernacle
For the alpha particle—
Atom or Aton what's the odds?
Radio the ether for the newest gods.

Saint Maxwell and Saint Whitehead
Pray for us . . .
                Grow up, ye bald heads.

Under the Guadarrama in the spring
I heard the nightingales in the ragged park
Where no queens walk as once they walked
Thinking with the silent tears queens dare not
    shed
Of childhood and a distant gayer land.

But shrieking jays silenced the nightingales
And drunken reds came shouting from the futból
Tearing down blossoms and rooting up the
    flowers,
And I never learned what the dead queens tried
    to say.
But I think the Hapsburg queens were glad to
    die.

Escorial . . .
There I have seen and you may see
Osiris-worship after all these ages,
Still the old frantic fear of the natural end,
Still the old dream of life beyond the grave,
Still the old magic charms of stones and gold,
Incense and muttered words of power.

'You Greeks are children.'
'You fake Egyptians pretty senile.'

Green marble clamped with gold
Cheats the Hapsburg-Bourbon bones
Deep in the fetid vaults which turn one sick.

Cannibal Christians out on the spree

> *Eating their god to eternitee,*
> > *Fee, fi, fo, fum.*

11

Is it so hard for men to live together?
Were they so gentle in the Old Stone Age?
Why the broken forearms in Badarian graves?

—No, I won't go home and open a bottle of
   port,
I'll have this out with Fate.—

Must I love my fellow neighbours,
Must I palpitate in sickly earnest
For two thousand million spiteful apes?
Must I love the cabman and the coolie,
Butlers and Basutos, hairy Ainus,
Grinning Orientals, surly Prussians,
Lovely Hindu-Negro-Chinese-Caribs,
Tax collectors, Fascists, pimps and Scotchmen?

Bring me the lowest-browed gorilla,
Introduce me to the cheerful chimpanzee;
Arm-in-arm we'll chant the People's Flag,
Take degrees in proletarian culture
And be analysed by Doctor Jung. . . .

12

Sometimes in the evening
Through the mountain gorge below
An enormous ghost comes creeping,
Lifting a flat head on a sinuous neck,
Peering above the highest peaks, and after

Slowly pulls its huge and misty bulk.

Awful devouring brute! And, ghost-like,
Indifferent to all mortal arms and threats,
It swallows up the valleys, crushes out
The tiny forests, and its floating mass
Comes nearer, nearer.
                              One by one
The distant houses vanish, and it comes
Horribly deliberate up the dimming slope,
Until a greyness settles on my sight
And even the scarlet dahlias are drab—
All weirdly lost in that terrific ghost.

An ancient terror chills me;
When these heaved-up rocks were mud and
     sand
Of a lost warm sea, at evening in the shallows
Enormous lizard-fishes came groping after
     prey,
Powerful stupid and cruel.
And all life fled from them until they starved
And set the world free for a nobler growth.

I sit in the belly of the mist ghost
Like Jonah in his whale wondering
Whether the gods love evil and ugliness
Or have no power or no goodwill to us,
Or whether Herakleitos saw the truth—
That strife is harmony and everything
Lives through its opposite—
So men must live their eras as lizard-fishes
To learn in time—or is it, to re-learn?—
The wisdom and grace of nobler creatures,
Bulls and deer and horses.

We must mock at the brutish
And the false-hearted,
The hypocrite and the fool;
Mock at the great words
When the many mouths chew them to folly,
Mock at the great deeds
Whittled down to dull lessons.

But let us know that we shall wound ourselves.

We are the far off future
Of the distant past,
We are the noble race for whom they dreamed
   and died.

It was not we they loved,
It was not our lives they died for;
Like arrogant fathers with humble wives
They loved in us only themselves,
They died, not that we should live
But that they should live again in us.

Oh, distrust all Heroes and Saviours,
Oh, beware of the life-hungry Ancestors
Preying on us, wanting to live in us . . .

The stuff of the body is immortal;
Before birth it was and after death it is.
But the soul
The evil or lovely soul is mortal
As a flower or a rainbow.

There come more flowers
But never again that one bright flower

Plucked by your love to lie in her breast.

In the south in winter
When the sun hangs too low in the hard sky
And the night wind remembers the frozen snow,
The yellow soil crumbles and breaks
As the thin bright iris petals push through,
The fleurs-de-lys, stemless, honey-scented,
Soft as young lips where love is.

The 'soul' is a tainted word.
I give it back fresh to you
Like the honey-scented iris
Which is sweet for a day
In winter
In the South.

14

But flowers are the sex of plants
Sweet and delicate and fragile
Like the soul of the deep earth-creativeness
Which is not all beautiful
But brings forth hideous things
In slime and dung. . . .

The earth is indeed the Mother
But 'the terrible Mother' of all dreams,
A cannibal Saturn of a mother—
Yet I love her.
How deep she goes!
In the great broken mountains
You can see how deep.
But her depths are lifeless

Like the grey ooze depths of the sea.
Life is of the rind and the shallows.
In the dark pools of the earth caverns
Even the fishes go blind.
In the tomb of Tutankhamen
Even the microbes were dead.

Horrible shuddering end of the life quest!
Suppose they had brought him alive
Suppose their magic substances and rites
And charms had brought his Ka alive
Blinking new baby eyes in the muffled tomb—
How horrible to live for all those centuries
In a hot gold prison where even the air was dead
Thirty centuries of knowing death is death.

And then what happiness what sweet relief
What gushing of grateful tears
When at last he heard the muffled picks
And the cool killing air stabbed in
And he knew he could die at last,
Die from the living death at last,
At last be dissolved and flow back . . .

In art we know that achievement
Is not to work much but to work well,
And it is so with life—
Not to live long but to live greatly.

The reward of art is the doing;
The reward of life is the living . . .
The priest will sell you a guaranteed ticket
For a family pew in resurrection green
At the general non-stop Paradise scene,
And the business man will sell you a pup

Or a diamond mine or a share in Krupp,
And the stinks and physics and x-square mob
Will show you how the wheels go round, begob,
But . . .

Kiss her now, kiss her now,
Now, now,
If you want to live, if you want to live,
Sweet, sweet, sweet,
Kiss her now, now, now,
Sweet life, kiss her now, sweet, sweet
On the lips, oh now, don't wait,
  Kiss her now,
   Kiss her now,
    Kiss her now, Sweet Life.

Says the wild thrush
To the sleet
From the hawthorn bush.

15

In misery have I walked the streets of London
That rich proud city
Of the penurious and the humiliated.

An Etruscan tomb is gayer than London streets.

Sharp-lined and glinting
The traffic clots go curdling
Through the dark veins of the town
In sharp mechanistic spasms
Like the fierce bleeding of a great machine,
Breaking the rhythm of our blood
Until the soft swirl and lapse of Thames

Alone seem unreal.

Bombed and blackened
Drab as the totem of a giant slum
Thutmosis' obelisk expires.

Where are the white nymphs
of the fountains
sung to by the starlings
in Trafalgar Square?

Even in winter
There are lovely dawns
Over the gutters and the chimney pots
To break my heart.

Like a huge grey leech
The city sucks our lives.

Why need we ring it round
With marble fortresses of death
Beleaguering the living dead?

Grim monstrous lotus of the dirty Thames . . .

And like a fool I said the human soul
Is a honey-scented iris . . .

Horatio Stylites
Double-blind with soot
On your pillar of gypsum,
Hang us out another signal.

16

Below the crooked bridge at Brantôme
The water of the Dronne runs clear and cold
Past the old garden of the monks.
I walked there in the bright September evening,
My blood hot with a long dream of love
And passionate yearning for life, more life.
The fire of my thought was hot and sweet,
Hiding with its gold haze the soft greensward
And the grey-brown trickling stream,
The last roses and the heavy elms.

With a swift shock my dream abandoned me
And the haze of fire was torn clear
For under an old willow I saw
The body of a dead snake in the water.
It was so dead, so utterly inert and dead,
Lying there, softly swaying in the water
On its back with its dead white belly
Turned under water to the sun
In a long slack curve pale and flaccid
Like a piece of old bleached rope
Swaying softly dead under the sun.

Now what I thought there I cannot tell you
For it was both more and less than thought—
I saw the white belly of the dead snake
And I saw the body of a dead English soldier
Laid like a coloured statue on the fire-step
I saw and the same sickly smell came choking
The body of a young German officer
His face blue-grey like his uniform
I saw the rag-clothed skeletons of Loos
I saw my own body lying white and helpless
Belly turned to the sun

Gently swaying in the water
Under the sunlight where the snake lay
With all the queer taut snake-life gone limp and lost.

I was not afraid, it was a great peace.

I saw that which was the snake
And myself and those others
Softly dissolve and drift with the stream
Down to the Dordogne
Down to the Gironde
Down to the great rollers of the sea,
And return as rain or cloud or air
But never again as a crisp-gliding snake
Rustling its way over dried grasses,
Never again as a human soul
Avid for much living . . .

17

Up here in the still unconquered mountains
Which are the broken loins of forgotten worlds
All day the sun triumphs through thin clear air
Far off snow-dappled the long splintered crests
Silently divide the fugitive blue
And near at hand the small cold stream
Sparkles and dashes against the stones
Echoing loudly like a fountain in a still court-
    yard
Through the pastures of the silent valley.

And all the slopes glitter with coloured wings.

'Like flowers', I thought, 'like flowers on wings
They swoop and flutter round their rooted sisters

Because on such a day so hushed and bright
Aeons ago an idle god came here
And thrusting back his ruffled hair at ease
Saw the long slopes of motionless flowers
And said:
        "If only such had wings!" '

18

One by one they are fading
The old sacred places,
One by one they are trampled out
By the brutes and priests and hucksters
And that ignoble brood of the War.

My belly yearned for Sicily
So desolate in all her high places,
Treeless, blasted by torrent and swamp,
A desert of wheat and sulphur,
Unhappy, diseased.

Near Syracuse a few flowers—
On Mount Hybla a few stunted shrubs
A remnant sweet with honey-blossom,
All that was left of many acres
Many lovely acres of dawn-pink blossom
Hummed over by myriads of bees.

I could not bear it.
There is too much destruction
And always of beautiful and sacred things.
I wanted to lie down and shed tears
For the ravishing of Sicily,
Poor Persephone of an island
Raped by all the thugs of Europe.

Pillars of Hercules . . .

A white squall blew up from Cadiz
Coming out of Portugal
North-west from the uneasy Bay.

I stood on the last mountains of Europe
Gazing at the first mountains of Africa
Across the little straits
Where the puny liners crawled in whiffs of
    smoke,
Ceuta a pinch of pearl dust at my feet.

Far to the west the long slow heave
Of the huge Atlantic, slow slow heave
Like the enormous breathing of a god;
Far to the east in shining sunlight
Ripples upon ripples
The innumerable laughter of the mid-earth sea.

Lonely was the road
And silent the pungent slopes,
A sacred place still holy and unprofaned
After all the generations that have passed.

Why was I dumb?
Why could I not lift my arms
And cry aloud to the sacred ones
Earth Sea and Sun?

I was swept speechless
By a huge choking wave of life.
I knew it was folly and wickedness
To worship Christs and abstractions

And never to revere the real holy ones
Sun Sea and Earth.

The solid mountain at my feet
Bore me through space like a wave
A delicious wave of life.

It seemed I was not on the world's edge
But in the real centre of the earth
Between Egypt and the Western Isles
Feeling in a flash the long generations
From the first of the husbandmen
To the last of the machine men
And the first new men after the machines
They who shall revere again
Sea Sun and Earth.

That moment of pure life
Is worth my eternity of death.
Methought I saw, methought I felt,
Methought I knew . . .

All I had suffered was forgotten
All I had to suffer was discounted;
I knew that I had striven rightly
And that my deathless body was accepted
By Earth Sun and Sea.

I knew that I was one of the remnant of life-
    seekers
In the narrowing dwindling free spaces
Outside the prisons.

My little perishable soul
I bequeath to men
If it is any use to them.

But men and women
Before it is too late
Will you not draw back from greed
    and destruction
Ere the earth becomes a cruel desert
And the sea a sterile pollution
And the sun black with anger against
    you?

You are building up the world with
    prisons
For yourselves and your children,
You are rotten with death-worship.

I think you are dying,
All the more do I think it
Because you breed pallid millions
And try to drill them into health.

Nothing that is worth being
Can be learned by drill,
Nothing that is worth giving
Can be bullied into another.

But there is deep and delicate life
If only you can seek in patience
For the moment, and let it come to you
From Sun Earth and Sea.

When I think of the world of men and
    women
The world as it is
I bow my head in my arms
And lament destruction and greed.

But in myself I feel exquisitely alive,
Life flows through me,
In a touch beyond prayer I ask
That my life quest go on till I die,
Oh, let the Sun still be mine
And the undying Sea
And the Holy Earth!

NEW POEMS

A PLACE OF YOUNG PINES

Up here in the house it is like a battlefield
Where I struggle for ever with myself
And am only victorious by defeating myself.

Here too come voices and passions,
All that would urge me against myself
And draw out the perpetual conflict.
All that is uncertain, all that is unhappy,
All that is noisy, assault me here.

But sometimes I step from my room,
Walking quietly so that none shall hear me,
And go and stand in a place of young pines.

In winter it roars with heavy waters,
But now in summer it is dried up and silent.
Where ran the waters lie polished stones
And nooks of clean brown sand,
And above that are the stiff dead pine needles
And the rough stems of the young pines.

They are so still, they live so contentedly,
Holding the hard rock, going down into darkness,
And lifting such gay green plumes to the sun.
They do not argue, they do not talk of success,
And if they want to excel it is only in growing.

So for a little time I stand among the pines
Above the clean dry water-course
Where all sounds are hushed.
There I am at peace, there I am at one with all things.
But up here I am not at peace,
Never truly and wholly at one with all things.

And for that I yearn—to be at one, to be at peace.

Down there among the pines I am at peace;
Not questioning I accept and am accepted,
And live in peace of life.
But up here I doubt if there is peace of life;
And sorrowfully and in dismay I question myself,
Asking if what I seek is not rather the peace of death,
The lapse, the going forth, the peace
After all the waters have passed under the young
    pines.

A GRAVE

No name, but wild flowers
And the emblem which you chose
And now is yours for ever. . . .

How many thousands in the years to come
Will pass indifferently these common tombs,
Led by the memory of your glowing spirit
To gaze upon the stone above your bones.

Nothing I see, but blind and choked with tears,
Hurt by the wrongs and agonies you suffered,
I stumble from your grave, but through the pain
Feel the high triumph that you lived and died
Humble and noble and august and poor.

TO ONE DEAD

It is pleasant to me to know that I have done with you.
If I owed you a debt, I have paid it;
If I mistook you, I have set it right;
If you wronged me, I have obliterated the wrong.
And so we are quits and at peace.

You cannot say that I have betrayed you,
For what in you was sharp rippling flame
I have fostered, and what was dark smoke
Of evil and hatred and suspicion I have ignored.

I have dealt with you more kindly than I would be dealt by—
Is there any purer justice?

Nevertheless I am glad to be done with you,
To say: 'It is all finished',
And to wave a last, but never indifferent farewell.

DILEMMA

You asked me if you should still go adventuring
For more beauty, new lands, strange faces,
For other moons and suns over other cities
And seas and forests you have never beheld;
Or whether you should sit down quietly
And con over all you have gathered,
Fingering your memories, counting your spoils,
Letting each day pass without comment,
Indistinguishably, a day only, a passage of hours,
Without one blood-beat of discovery or pain?

How could I answer in words?
So I drew you silently to the window
Opening upon the spring twilight.
There was a deep orange afterglow from the sun,
And a young moon with a star in her hand,
The last swifts dashed screaming over the roofs
While the first bats swerved noiselessly across the
        square,
There was a murmur of talk and of moving feet
As people strolled and met after work,
A peasant's cart went by with a man driving
And a girl holding a candle in a paper shade,
And someone played a mandoline.

Were you answered? I do not know,
For after a long silence you spoke of other things.
But I do not know any other answer to give you.

JANUARY ACONITES

THE aconites twist and drag themselves
Up from the naked rainless earth,
And make little gold havens of petals
Among the grey clods under the stark snaky
   vines.

And if one day is trampled underfoot
Or another forced awry and another stunted,
Still there are days and days and golden days
Like aconite-stars under the grey heaven of
   olives.

MORNING IN THE SOUTH

THE morning, like a living crystal, blue,
Cloudless and deep . . .
      Some god has passed unseen
Leaving an ecstasy in wave and land
And fragrance of his body on the air,
A living hush, part awe, part tenderness,
The promise of the mystery of birth
Which seems more real than death.
        Could time stand still,
Poise with unswerving wing at this one hour
When life has stepped into immortal paths
And beauty triumphs like a faultless rose.
Could this sun stand for ever in this sky,
For ever pour forth pure morning light,
This faint warm wind for ever breathe, these boughs
For ever tremble with such greenery,
The air still hold its fragrance, and this sea
Shine like a richer sky to the last verge
Where both embrace. Why should not this endure,
This unexpected touch with kinder gods?

Because it passes it is beautiful.

DEATH OF ANOTHER HERO

Who is this that is borne with lamentation,
Who is this that is honoured by a proud people?
Is it one who gave life and hope?
Is it one who gave knowledge, wisdom or beauty?
Is it one who died that others might live?
Who is this hero? Let me know,
Let me share in the sorrow of my nation
And lay my wreath of praise on a worthy tomb.

It is the rich man who is dead at last,
Struck—Nemesis!—in the very brain
Which plotted all that senseless gathering.
Gone! Like a beggar, like a frowsty worm
Trodden beneath the contemptuous foot of Death.

It is the rich man, he who spent the years,
All lovely hours or dark, to gather more,
And yet more, and yet more, and more and more,
He who possessed, who was feared, who was hated,
Crucified himself between conceit and fear,
Now boasting of his power like a loud pimp
Bullying a frightened woman, and anon,
His eyes darkened and narrowed with fear,
Dreading in abject bowel-shaken terror
The speechless vengeance of the wronged.

It is the rich man, peak-quotation Judas,
Who for five hundred million silver pieces
Sold life and his fellow men,
But first and last and every day himself,
And with each shilling bought a sullen fear,
The fear of losing it.

Now all are lost.

Ring out, base bugles! Sound, ye empty drums!
Stand to attention, low Servility,
Lick-spittle Flattery, whining Parasites!
Your hero passes. Stand with palms reversed
And pockets inside out.
And you, gaunt legions of the too-honoured slain,
Rise from your geometric lines of graves,
Kindle in empty sockets the fierce fires
Of your avenging eyes, stare from your shrouds,
There goes your general to his last unrest,
There trails one corpse which made you corpses too.

1933

Now one by one the nobler fires die down,
Trampled by brutal feet: and now
Where light once glowed
Black smoking ashes mark our murdered hopes.
Ever the music fades, the vision trembles
Until we know not if it lives
Or quivers, a spent mirage, in our hearts,
While fainter, fainter sound the trembling chords
Which led us to the dwelling of the gods.

O smouldering darkness of the universal hate,
O ignorant clamour which has killed the music,
O base destruction of the turreted vision!

I mourn, I mourn alone for a world dying;
In vain I yearn for a world to be born.

Accuse not the gods, the eternal powers.
As of old they remain, and are just.
If they shatter the things they have made,
They are just.
Seek not for rest—it shall not be granted.
For us there can be no rest,
Though we dreamed of the peace of achieve-
   ment,
Never doubted young hearts and your strength
Would be spent in our aid.

They have not come, they will not come.

O remnant sore-tried, O weary ones,
Close the ranks,
The long battle is not ended nor the contest won—
Close the ranks—
We are beaten but we are not crushed—
Close the ranks—
Our noblest are gone, our heroes dead—
Close the ranks—
Fight on in the battle eternal,
Of mind and spirit against force and hate,
Close the ranks,
Fight on.

LIFE GOES ON

Let not your life become a Pharaoh's tomb
Of buried memories, hopes embalmed,
Shut in hot airless silence
Where day by day nothing stirs, nothing lives,
Gold in the darkness never gleams,
The drugged soul broods in a passive swoon
Sightless over unseen treasures softly rotting
In the hot darkness through dusty months.

Youth may be furnished like a king
With crystal dream and golden ecstasies,
But when the proud king leaves for a far journey
And is lost in the cold wake of the world
In starry seas, the lively palace
Sinks dark and sullen as a tomb.

Let the rain and wind of tears and sighs storm through it,
With swift wreckage tarnishing the gold,
With lightning of despair and long low thunder
Of the world's sorrow, until the tomb is broken
And the moon gleams through.

Mourn not for the wreckage, but as the moon fades
In the quick dawn, break from the ruins,
For life goes on.
                    Taste then the morning air
However bitter and however cruel,
Receive in nakedness those darts of light
Whether in kindness or in anger thrown,
Tread humbly on the sacred breast of earth,
And grasp revered water's touch.

Oh, no more gold and crystal in high rooms,
But rain-washed rock and tender fugitive water
Under the old sky worshipped with new eyes,
For life goes on.

THE CRYSTAL WORLD

THE CRYSTAL WORLD

ONE
Nile-lotus among women, dear flower of girls,
Exquisite as a slender dark hibiscus,
Take my head on your young breasts, beloved,
Touch my cheek with your delicate hands
And—break, O my heart, break with longing.

TWO
Now I am lonely and silent as a sea-cave
Emptied of the cool life-giving waters
That filled me with echoes of murmuring gladness.
Tide follows tide; ah! will she come to me
Awaiting in passionate suspense my life-giver?

THREE
Nefertiti, the young queen-goddess, was beautiful.
Egypt lived happy, looking upon her.
There lives now one beautiful as Nefertiti,
Tender and slim as a young reed in blossom,
And 'I love you' I murmur as she passes.

FOUR

I shall remember these undying days
In the waste places of life
And in the narrow pass of death
I shall remember one young delicate face
And the clear frank eyes that smiled
And looked love at me,
And the sensitive lips that kissed me,
And the soft dark hair.
I shall remember the fine hands
That held my life so tenderly,
And the woman breasts
That moved me to such yearning.

These I shall remember,
But above all that this woman's soul
Reached out to mine, and we seemed one
And there was an end of all loneliness.
In solitude and in the last twilight
This I shall remember.

FIVE

Now night and morning I say 'Yes' to life,
Not doubtfully, nor in hurt defiance,
But swiftly and in truth. . . .

Too swift the hours upon this crest of life—
O *lente, lente currite,* the lover's cry,
The scholar's plea, Ovid and Faust:
Give me more time, more time!
Ah! let me know and taste
The sweetness and the glory of her love. . . .

We are in a great city of many men,
City of greed and bitter want,
Of much madness and a little pleasure.
Footsteps of men, voices, strange sounds
Of machines are about us; strange eyes,
Strange faces, flicker and pass.
We hear, and hear not; see, and see not.
Out of our love we have built a crystal refuge
Unseen but very strong and ours,
Only we can enter it and be safe.
We dwell at the very heart of life. . . .

O my love, my perfect one,
My almond-tree suddenly in bloom,
My tender wild-bird with the clear eyes,
White nymph of southern waves,
And flower, bright flower of life!
To die for you were too small a gift;
I shall live for you.

SIX

O world of strange and violent men,
Let us have our world!

It is a world which has no battlefield,
No factions and no bitter strife for power,
And scarcely touches yours.

Give us our world, and in the days to come
It shall enrich your children's children,
Our world where dawn blooms like a cyclamen
Over the wooded hills and whispering sea,
With roses and the rustling of vine leaves
And sun upon the sands and ancient towns
And all the lovely things that men have made
And all simplicity and truth and trust
Set as our jewels in the gold of love!

This is our glory, this our power,
For this we cast your blood-stained world
    away—
Give us our world, ah, do not harm
So fragile and so sweet a thing
That, could you enter it,
Beauty would enter all your tortured flesh
And happy tears wash bright your maddened
    eyes.

You are the power and glory of your world;
But we, we are little, we are humble,
You will never know that we have gone away
Into that crystal world we make together.

Ah, let us have our world.

SEVEN
Madam, Miss Otis regrets....

The waiter tips the ash-tray, dusts the cloth,
Sicilian exile. New York melody
Flatters his gangster ears—Simonides
You know, is dead, and dead Empedocles....

No, this is too much pain, this is not true,
Those words have not been said, were never said,
It cannot be those eyes look hurt and cold.

Go catch a falling star, go climb a tree,
Go, go....

        It seems I also have to learn
Undreamed of pain, having so lately learned
Undreamed of happiness. This room's my School.
For what? For Scandal? No, for breaking hearts
And learning how to like it. Yes. And yes

Madam, Miss Otis regrets.

EIGHT
Give me the grace to love her perfectly....

O bitter heart, be sweet, be sweet for once;
Forget your dead, forget the years of hell,
Forget that there is anything but love.

Your sun of life goes flaming to its doom;
Be thankful for it; think, you might have died
Like common men who deal in pounds and stocks,
Poor sensual men who never came alive.

347

But you have lived, have known the ecstasy,
Have touched her hand, have kissed her lips, have
  looked
Your life into her eyes. O heart, be still;
Be still, you longing for the greater joy.
The greater joy is giving all to her,
Yes! Though it break you, bitter heart of pride.

Mountains and southern sea, great silent woods,
Full moon and crescent, stars of my Provence,
Spring flowers and autumn scents and summer suns,
Beautiful world which I have loved indeed,
In this my need, be kind.
                        You hope too much.

The Roman fountains—would she not love them?
Blue Nemi in its cup of hills, the wine
And olives; Firenze, ah, Firenze,
Who woke my youth to beauty, you who bore
Dante and Petrarch. . . .
                        Yearning heart, be still;
Be humble; it is not given to you
To give her all your world; that golden key
Slips from your fingers.
                        Learn to stand aside,
To smile at pain, and murmur as you die:

'I had the grace to love her perfectly'.

NINE
Misery, ah, misery of the endless hours,
In the daytime, in the night, unending hours,
All the hours of my death.

What shall be garnered from the barren sea?
What shall I gather from my barren days?

I knew there had to be an end to joy,
But never guessed the hand I loved
Must stab me into misery.

Darling, I must, I do apologise—
I had a kind of zest for living
And am too long a-dying.
Leave all the rest unpardoned
But forgive me that.

TEN

Let it winter now forever,
Let there be no more sun and flowers;
Let the unkind wind be all I gather;
My love the foam of a foreign sea.

Sweetheart, sweetheart, your hand stabbed me,
So death will be sweet when it comes, too late,
Too late, for I might have died with your kisses
Still warm on my mouth, and your love in my eyes.

ELEVEN

This strange sad beauty of the ruined South
Speaks to my ruined heart
And echoes through my empty life.

Hot blue sky in December
Over the huge sad marshes
Where the slim cranes brood
Among the dead reeds and dead water,
Hot sky over the fields

Of dead corn-stalks and dead plants,
Oh, irony of clear blue sky
Over the gaunt dead trees
Bearded with grey sinister moss—
Laughing sky of youth and life
Over a dead, a ruined, a murdered land.

I walked over the rare grass
Beneath the noble ilex trees
And looked at the happy white house
And heard the clear young laughter;
I knew, at that moment of peace I knew
I should never see her again,
Never again look into those clear eyes
Which moved me so deeply,
Never again hear her fresh young laughter
Which for those few sweet days
Brought me out of the house of the dead,
Never again, never again.

The anguish of it hurt my flesh,
And the bitter irony of that young sky
So beautifully indifferent
To the dead ruined earth. . . .

'*Leave them only their eyes*. . . .'

TWELVE
There shall be no reproach from me,
No word of bitterness or scorn;
To live alone with so much grief
Breaks every passion save regret.

O passionate regret for hours
That shone like mountains tipped with fire,

That seemed to be the dawn and were
But embers of a dying sun.

O passionate regret! Can Time,
That crushes us with heavy hours,
Abate no moment of this pain
Nor quench that yearning of the flesh?

THIRTEEN

Hide from me all lovely things
Whether of skies or starry flowers.
Let me not see the grace of women
Nor look in children's eyes.

Give me things harsh and cruel
In a grim derelict land,
For these can only kill
While beauty tortures alive.

FOURTEEN

Punctual as waking comes my grief,
And every solitary hour
Hurts me with memories of you.

All music brings you to my mind
And every flower you might have worn;
And silent amid laughter I
Bitterly hear your laughter too.

So that I long to sleep, but sleep
Is bitterest of all, for there
You come to me in dreams, and smile,
Saying 'I love you' . . .
                              and I wake to tears.

FIFTEEN

I tried to give you all I had, but you
Asked only two, the costliest, gifts. I gave
Absence and silence: Now be happy, dear.

SIXTEEN

I shall not need to labour for you, dear,
Nor give my days to make your days secure;
Nor ever will my hand be laid in love
Upon you in the womb, never my lips
Shall kiss the sacred mother-flesh that breeds you.

I shall not need to anguish for you both
In time of travail, waiting with strained eyes
To know your dear life has not harmed a dearer.
Nor shall I ever steal towards a bed
To watch you sleeping by your sleeping mother.

I shall not need to make you lullabies,
For you will never wake, my dearest, never;
Nor once be jealous that your baby mouth
Commands the tender breasts I wooed with kisses,
Nor once be happy that your eyes have smiled.

I shall not need to mourn that you must die,
For you will never live, poor nameless phantom,
Dreamed out of nothing by a foolish heart.
My paper children, stored on silent shelves,
Shall—live for ever?—crumble into dust.

O comrades lying in the fields of France,
Strange is our fate; childless like me you died;
For us the coloured flame of love fades out,
The million generations have an end,
The ship of life sinks in a dusky sea.

SEVENTEEN

Grief is profuse of words;
But Happiness goes shyly,
With muted lips, demurely,
And a sweet unconscious smile.

Out of despair and sorrow,
From the borderland of death,
A brave and noble woman
Has raised me up to life.

Grant me the grace to love her
As she would have me love,
And find me words to utter
The joy she brings to birth.

EIGHTEEN

New blossoms for my love, give me new flowers,
Every fresh bud of the scarce-wakened spring,
Then late spring flowers and summer-scented roses
That hide the kiss of sunlight in their hearts
As I in mine the sweetness of your love.

NINETEEN

All that I have is bought
By the price of my words and dreams.

Now on the brink of joy
As I hurry to meet my love
This fancy comes to my mind:
Henceforth my darling will go

Clad in my words and dreams,
From the silk at her tender breasts
To the silk that clasps her knee,
From the necklace about her throat
To the little shoes on her feet.

I shall think when I see her walk
With her eyes so alive with love:
'How proudly my dear one moves
Clad in her lover's dreams'.

TWENTY
Never, never may I feel such anguish
Eating at my life and flesh as when I
Thought I must no more see you nor
Touch your lovely body nor hear you—
Ah! my love, my love, be tender with me.

TWENTY-ONE
Heavy the night sky,
Stinging sharp the rain,
And in the Atlantic gloom
The cruel innumerable waves
Threaten with furious foam. . . .

But, ah, in me is peace
And sunlight and the scent
Of southern hillsides,
Stars kissing tranquil water,
The song of evening birds,
Fruit trees in blossom. . . .

Beloved I go to her I love. . . .

TWENTY-TWO

I

What is poetry? And what is love?
Dead words of a dying epoch
Which leave a vague distaste
Though one has to use them
Since the new words have not yet come to birth.

Poetry? The dust of learned manuals,
Ghost words of metaphysics,
The newest critic with the newest views?
The see how smart I am, how well-informed,
How rare my feelings?
The see me contemplate myself in Nature?

And love? In shilling magazines?
In theories of the Unbewusst?
Records of Sapphism in New York State?

II

Brood on the fate of men and women,
That flicker of forgotten days and nights
Which makes a life once lived.

Under the rows of headstones drilled with names
Where are the poets and the passionate lovers?

But the ripple of dull slow days
May break in a sudden leap of glittering foam,
And the light diffused burn to one diamond point.
And whether in mockery or envy or regret,
We say: 'They were lovers;
He was a poet'.

And leave it at that as the gong rings for dinner.

III

Now whether these two I write of really lived
Or whether I 'made them up' as I walked
And dawdled under the cypress and arbutus
Listening to the nightingales
And the lap of a crystal sea—
Does it matter?

                      Zaïre, vous pleurez—
He had that moment, the cynical old man
With the lean sardonic grin.
Dido still builds her pyre,
Juliet calls to her tassel-gentle,
Héloïse rides with Abélard to the Loire. . . .

They are mine. I have brought them
To whatever life-in-words they have.
They are part of me, yet part of the changing world,
Me and Not-me.

                 He and She
Just as much You as I,
Or anyone who lives their pain and bliss.

IV

Now the 'story' behind these poems
Is very simple and very usual,
The kind of thing that often happens
And will go on happening
Until the feelings and impulses
Of men and women are wholly changed.

And it is waste of time to start guessing
What people will do in Utopia
Ten thousand years hence;

Just as it is waste of time
To be morally shocked, and say:
'They ought not to have done this'.
The point is they did do it;
And what matters is Why?, not How?

Why is it that from time to time
In this queer chaotic routine of life
Two people are impelled to each other
With a force they are powerless to resist?
Not for a mere sexual experience,
Not for the ordinary formal marriage,
But against all the social rules?
Nothing matters except to be together,
To have the two lives merge in one.
When they separate they live in feverish misery
Counting the minutes until their next meeting.
When they are together they are supremely alive,
The smallest happenings are vivid and significant,
Life is no longer formless but finely shaped
In patterns of inexplicable beauty.
Inexplicable. It is inexplicable.
We cannot say why, but it happens.
And, according to our mood, we say:
'There are two most happy lovers';
Or 'There go a couple of fools';
Or 'We can't ask *them* to dinner again'.
And much they care whatever we may say!

V

The passion at first is hardly sexual at all,
But—by instinct or convention?—
Speaks in terms of 'this is beautiful'.
Not in the subtle forms of the artist

Who is always seeking exact equivalents
For the experiences of the sensibility,
But in the common terms of common men—
She is flowers, the sea, a young queen,
Primitive symbols.
The emotions are intense, not subtle,
In no way intellectualised.
What he seeks is an ecstasy and a peace—
The strange ecstasy of being together
So that they create their 'crystal world'
Which is only the common world made vivid;
The deep peace of being at one.

You must not confuse these little poems,
The attempt to express these feelings,
With the feelings themselves.
You must believe them to be utterly sincere
And flowering from the whole nature of both.
(Is it as Lenin priggishly said
A mere matter of biology and culture?
Suppose you can state the relation
In terms of ova and spermatazoa
And of civilised companionship?
Why just that one person
When so many are available?
Just bourgeois sentimentality?
But the bourgeois are against it!
And admire the ingenuity of Sapiens
Who can make biology into a life poem!)

You see, for them it is not enough
To have a biological affair—
Which would be quite easy—
Or to meet as intimate friends,
Which would be even easier.

You have here two passionate natures
Unable to compromise
Under the smug winking of the hypocrite world.
They must have everything,
Must share each day and night,
Must grow together closer, closer,
And build their 'crystal world'.

VI

But there are obstacles, there always are.
(No need to quote from Shakespeare.)
Never mind what obstacles, but say:
'The Bishops and the Bench would not approve,
Nor would the T.U.C., nor Mrs Grundy,
Nor Mr Grundy putting on the green'.

Therefore, this ecstatic bliss,
This rash, this unadvised, this sudden bliss
Is soon shot through with pain.
There seems no help for it but to renounce,
To part for ever, with one brutal stroke
Cut through the delicate filaments
Already binding them together.

Useless to dream of what they might have done,
How all this beautiful world if lived together
Would seem so beautiful, and lived alone
Not worth the living.
Passion's defeatism!
'Give us our world!' Or nothing.
Mad with pain and all regret
They smash their crystal world
And part for ever.

VII

It's not so easy. . . .

It is not easy to turn back
From the young dawn of happiness,
To tear asunder with most exquisite pain,
To face this double suicide of life,
To know that the days hereafter
Will be grey ashes of time.
Does it need an analysis à la Proust
To show their tragic grief?

Imagine them parted, then,
Each in an infernal twilight of despair.
Unknown to her, he is at sea,
Wretchedly fighting the enemy hours,
With only one aim—to go far away,
To be as many miles away as possible,
To shun the damnable pain-bliss
Of all that might evoke the thought of her.
And thinks about her all the more
And broods his bitter grief.

And she? No sooner has he gone,
Taken her at her word, and gone,
Than the sublime good sense of women
Whispers that this is treachery to life.
Is she not the life-giver,
The bearer of new life?
She, female-linked in the flesh
To the remotest birth of life,
Knows that each ancestress in turn
Dared all that life might be.
This is real,
The obstacles an evil dream,

Sheer whimsies of men's crazy brains
Inventing new self-tortures.

Driven by that terrific force
Deep in the chemistry of her flesh,
She hurries haggard-eyed and trembling
Through the rain and murk of the city,
Seeking, seeking, Isis seeking for Osiris,
Rebuffed from unfriendly doors, humiliated—
Is her face wet with rain or tears?—
Seeking, seeking, and does not find.
He has gone.
Paolo and Francesca drift in hell
But drift together.
These, by their own too tortured will
Drift each in a separate hell.

VIII

In the poems of separation
You may read their grief.
And for a moment think:
These are not mere words of a writer
But the clumsy stammerings of pain,
It really was like that, it did happen,
That misery and agony were real.
Their lives had broken into death.
All about them was unreal,
A misty phantasm of dim figures.
All their consciousness
Was the long agony of absence,
And in their flesh that unceasing pain
Over the contracted heart.

How could it end?

It is a strange perversity
To think that the modern world of applied science
Must be less vivid and dramatic
Than the old slow ignorant world.
Only the dull routine mind thinks these things dull,

And it would be dull and unmoved in Athens or
    Arcady.
There is no need to write Pindaric odes
To ocean liners and cable companies,
Only to accept such things as part of life,
Good or bad according as they are used;
And to realise that in this crisis of two lives—
So utterly unimportant to the rest of the world
But to them the very pivot of existence—
This unbearable strain of unhappy separation
Could not have been resolved so swiftly
But for the much-despised gifts of Science.

You must imagine him thousands of miles away
From the place of their last meeting,
All those days like a vast fog of silence between
    them.
Day follows slow day in brooding misery
As he says farewell to the hope and sunlight of
    life
And mourns for an unborn child,
Since in this strange condition of humanity
Only with one person can he feel enough hope
To dare that grave adventure of renewing life
Begun so long ago in primæval seas.
Great is our terror of the civilisation
Men have built up in such confusion,
Terrible our dread that another self
May be born to suffer as we suffered;

Only the deep hope of an inexplicable passion
Can triumph over it.

So the days die, but the pain does not die.

One morning as usual he walks out
Through that queer landscape of desolate marsh
And tangled second-growth woods
Bearded with grey-blue Spanish moss,
Where the turkey-buzzards wheel overhead
And the graceful cranes wade among reeds.
He pauses to watch the brilliant flitting
Of two bright red cardinal birds,
And sighs that beauty is no more beautiful;
And then returns to the house.

Lying on the table is a Western Union cable
With his name on it—two cables.
He picks them up listlessly, thinking:
'New Year's greetings from friends in New
    York';
Opens one carelessly as he walks to meet his
    hostess
And reads:
'Have decided to be with you come and fetch
    me',
And then her name.

Just that. And it changed the world, their world,
Brought back the crystal world.

                    x
In a sense the 'story' ends here,
The long crisis of pain and absence is ended,

The wild effort at renouncing is a failure
Through some inner power in both
Stronger than their conscious wills.
They cannot not be together.
At whatever cost or condemnation
They must work out the life-pattern between
    them.

We might leave it at that, but inevitably
Comes the query: 'And what happened next?'
The public is never satisfied
Until lovers are safely buried
Or somehow cornered into disaster,
Until these queer disturbing people
Can be ticketed and pigeon-holed,
And the safe routine go on.
I shall not bury them, but I shall be brief.

You must imagine that he turns pale, icy pale,
As if his blood were frozen with the shock of joy.
Without strength to stand he drops into a chair
Fumbling with shaking fingers at the other cable
While his hostess, unseen, gazes wide-eyed.
At last it tears open and—anti-climax—
Is a message about 'business',
Therefore incomprehensible and of no importance.

Then, though the whole being is in turmoil,
The 'soul' as it were sobbing in a paroxysm of
    relief,
The impulse to action, the will to plan, assert
    themselves.
There is a swift hunt for liner sailings;
A long run by car against the clock

To get an answering cable through that day;
A long hallucinated evening
Of talk and planning with a friend;
A long, long tedious journey by rail
To the great city, and a queer long day
Of waiting and more cables and a cinema not
    seen
And talk with friends not remembered,
And one touch of woman's spite—laughed at—
In the last farewells on the steamer.

Endless days and nights at sea
As the ship shuddered through storm and rain,
Infinite sleepless hours
Trying to adjust to this unhoped-for happiness
While the wind shrieked in the ventilator,
Mad panics that Something or Somebody
Would intervene to prevent it,
Hour upon hour upon hour upon hour
Of mad impatience to be there,
To be together,
To find peace after the torture.

And that too ends, and they meet at last,
Almost speechless, moving slowly hand-in-hand,
A little bowed with the weight of so much
    passion,
But at one and at peace for ever.

And, yes, together they saw the Roman fountains,
And together looked at Perseus and David,
And together slept under the stars of Provence;
And beauty was far more beautiful together
Than they had dreamed in the far-off days of
    torture. . . .

'Give us our world.'
It will not be given; you must make it.
Only from the purity of extreme passion,
And, alas, the purity of extreme pain,
Can you build the crystal world.